PERFUME

LALIQUE

BOTTLES

PERFUME
LALIQUE
BOTTLES

Mary Lou and Glenn Utt
with Patricia Bayer

CROWN PUBLISHERS, INC.
New York

Design by Nancy Kenmore

The authors gratefully acknowledge Alfred A. Knopf, Inc. for permission to excerpt from *Perfume* by Patrick Süskind. Copyright © 1985.

Published by Crown Publishers, Inc., 201 East 50th Street, New York, New York 10022

CROWN is a trademark of Crown Publishers, Inc.

Manufactured in Japan

Library of Congress Cataloging-in-Publication Data
Utt, Mary Lou.
Lalique perfume bottles/Mary Lou and Glenn Utt with Patricia Bayer; introduction by Marie-Claude Lalique.
p.   cm.
Bibliography: p.
Includes index.
1. Lalique, René, 1860–1945—Catalogs. 2. Lalique, Cristal—Catalogs. 3. Perfume bottles—France—History—20th century—Catalogs. I. Utt, Glenn. II. Bayer, Patricia. III. Title.
NK5198.L44A4 1989
748.8′2′0924—dc19   88-25754
ISBN 0-517-57191-9
10 9 8 7 6 5 4 3 2 1
First Edition

CONTENTS

DE SON VIVANT RENÉ LALIQUE ETAIT DÈJÁ UNE LÉGENDE. Bien que tout cela m'échappait lorsque j'étais petite fille, pour moi il était simplement grand-père. Le Patriarche de la famille qui accrochait aux murs de sa chambre mes dessins d'enfant. Je n'avais pas à l'esprit à cette epoque lá, qu'un jour j'aurai la charge d'assumer sa renommée.

Au nom de mon grand-père est associé l'art décoratif l'un des plus visuel de ce siècle. Les historiens dans l'ensemble reconnaissent que le point crucial au depart de sa réputation de "verrier" à son association avec François Coty. René Lalique était reconnu pour ses créations de bijoux au moment de la Belle Epoque. Le verre jusqu'en 1906 n'est pas son seul centre d'intérêt, jusqu'au moment où M. Coty emménage dans de luxueux locaux voisins à la boutique de mon grand-père, Place Vendôme.

Une association lucrative s'ensuie entre les deux hommes et une page nouvelle dans l'histoire du verre est tournée. Quand les flacons de René Lalique pour François Coty font leur première apparition, non seulement ils vont révolutionner la présentation des parfums mais aussi marquer la réelle naissance de mon grand-père dans le monde verrier.

Nôtre Société dessine et fabrique des flacons de parfum depuis cette époque. Mon père Marc, a par exemple, réalisé les fameux flacons pour Nina Ricci, et je continue moi-même de créer flacons dans le cadre de nôtre Société. On peut donc dire que la contribution de Lalique dans le monde des Arts Décoratifs est notament lié au développment des flacons à parfum.

Malheureusement, très peu de documents éclairent cette partie de l'oeuvre de René Lalique. Pratiquement la totalité des archives de nôtre usine ont été détruites durant la deuxième guerre mondiale. Je suis donc particulièrement reconnaissante du travail de recherche qu'ont effectué Mary Lou et Glenn Utt et Patricia Bayer pour leur précieuse contribution à cet aspect de l'oeuvre familiale. Après tout je suis moi-même assidue collectioneur des flacons de mon grand-père et une partie de ma collection personnelle est illustrée dans les pages suivantes. Les Utts' propre collection reste cependant l'une des plus belle de leur genre. Elle est l'initiale inspiration de ce livre. La passion de Monsieur et Madame Utt pour Lalique leur a donné la curiosité et l'énergie nécessaire pour réaliser ce formidable projet. Et c'est ce haut niveau de connaissance et d'expertise qui permettra à la renommée de René Lalique de ce perpetuer dans les temps.

Marie-Claude Lalique

RENÉ LALIQUE WAS A LEGEND EVEN IN HIS OWN LIFETIME. But all this escaped me when I was a little girl. He was simply "Grandpa." He was the patriarch of the family who proudly tacked my childhood drawings onto the walls of his bedroom. It never occurred to me that someday I would become the caretaker of his legacy.

My grandfather's name is synonymous with one of the most extraordinary decorative vocabularies of this century. Art historians might argue that the critical link in his development as a *verrier* was his association with François Coty. René Lalique was first acclaimed as a purveyor of elegant jewelry for the tastemakers of the Belle Époque. Glass was not his paramount concern until roughly 1906, about the time Coty moved into elegant new quarters next to my grandfather's boutique on the Place Vendôme.

A lucrative association between these great men ensued and consequently a new chapter in the history of glass was written. When René Lalique's flacons for Coty first appeared, they not only revolutionized the manner in which fragrance was packaged and purchased but also marked my grandfather's full-fledged entry into the world of glass.

Our company has been designing and manufacturing scent bottles ever since. My father, Marc, for example, created the famed flacons for many Nina Ricci fragrances, and I continue to design and manufacture bottles and other boudoir items for Cristal Lalique. Therefore, if we are to understand my family's contributions to the decorative arts, one must certainly address this particular chapter of our esthetic development.

Unfortunately, few documents shed light on this aspect of René Lalique's *oeuvre*. Much of the archival material at our Wingen glassworks was destroyed during World War II. I therefore am grateful to Mary Lou and Glenn Utt and Patricia Bayer for their immeasurable contribution to the literature on the subject. After all, I too am an ardent collector of my grandfather's flacons, and many from my collection are illustrated in this handsome volume. The Utts' collection of scent bottles, however, is perhaps one of the finest of its kind. It provided the impetus for the book. And Mr. and Mrs. Utts' passion for Lalique imbued them with the requisite energy, patience, and curiosity to complete what turned into a truly formidable project. Only through their brand of scholarship can we intelligently and cohesively ensure that René Lalique's legacy will endure.

English translation by B. J. Santerre

The

S W E E T E S T

E S S E N C E S . . . .

are always
contained in
the smallest glasses.

————◆————

John Dryden

PREFACE

THE ESSENCE OF PERFUME IS JUST THAT—ITS FRAGRANCE—ever alluring, yet intangible and evanescent. But there is a longer-lasting significance in the packaging of a scent, and some of the strongest, most artistic messages were conveyed in the glass bottles of French designer René Lalique (1860–1945). In his long, rich, and profitable career, the goldsmith-turned-glassmaker created tens of thousands—indeed, millions—of *objets d'art,* from sparkling Art Nouveau jewels to pearly opalescent glass vases to figural relief panels to his various and wonderful flacons, by far the most numerous of his creations.

Today the art glass perfume bottles of René Lalique, as well as those of the still-thriving family firm, Cristal Lalique—run by his son, Marc, until his death in 1977 and today by Marc's daughter, Marie-Claude Lalique—are highly sought after by discerning collectors, fetching impressive sums in auction houses and antiques shops in New York, London, Paris, Tokyo, and elsewhere. Like-wise, museums and galleries covet and display Lalique bottles—in both their permanent collections and in temporary exhibitions—and numerous books and articles on Art Deco, on perfume bottles, and on the man himself have included Lalique's flacons and thus helped increase interest in and spread the legacy of this creative genius.

This first book to be devoted to Lalique perfume bottles not only provides ample background on the art and creativity of René Lalique concerning his massive perfume bottle output but it also illustrates, for the first time, all of his and Cristal Lalique's known flacons. It includes those that were sold empty by the Lalique firm and by other retailers as well as those that were custom-designed and made by Lalique for the scents of French *parfumeurs,* including Coty, Guerlain, Houbigant, Roger et Gallet, and American fashion stores, such as Saks Fifth Avenue and Jay-Thorpe Co. of New York and Alexander and Oviatt of Los Angeles.

Company records do not exist before 1921 and from that date until recently are sketchy at best. Thus, the task of compiling the 288 unduplicated flacon designs produced from 1908 to the present was, to say the least, a formidable one requiring several years of research. Almost as challenging was the detective work necessary to assemble the illustrations from around the world.

The research encompassed the review of all literature, auction catalogs over the last twelve years, information from the leading dealers, viewing of twenty major private collections, and essentially all recent museum showings, as well as interviews with perfume company officials, auction house specialists, museum curators, and, of course, executives of Cristal Lalique. We have excluded some scent bottles that *may* be of Lalique design and we are certain that more will be found in the coming years. Certainly, errors will come to light as the total body of knowledge expands.

The Appendix includes a summary listing of all Lalique perfume bottle designs, including information relating to company, size(s), signature type, relative rarity and value, as well as pertinent comments and an explanation of the codes and criteria used in the cataloging.

An overview of the rich variety of scent containers throughout the ages is also included and the importance of the French perfume industry examined, from its eighteenth-century roots to its early twentieth-century efflorescence—this in part due to Lalique's genius—to its present prestigious role in the world's ever eager and still fast-growing market.

René Lalique's place in the pantheons of both Art Nouveau and Art Deco design is paramount, but so is his contribution to the modern fragrance industry by way of his handsome glass packaging for scents. This book, we hope, makes this fact abundantly and beautifully clear—in both words and, even more valuable, in pictures.

PERFUME

LALIQUE

BOTTLES

CHAPTER 1

René Lalique

RENÉ LALIQUE WAS BORN IN THE SMALL TOWN OF Äy in France's Champagne district on April 6, 1860. He was the only child of a vendor of small novelty goods, a man about whom little is known and who died when René was in his late teens. His mother's family hailed from his birthplace, which is in northeast France on the northern bank of the Marne, near Reims, some twelve miles (twenty kilometers) north. The family moved to the borders of Paris two years after René's birth but subsequently returned to the lovely countryside for many holidays.

The youngster René received his primary education in the eastern Paris suburb of Vincennes at the Lycée Turgot, where he won an award for drawing in 1871. Indeed, he was known to have excelled at drawing from nature from an early age, and a family story reveals Lalique's early entrepreneurial and artistic skills with his successful sale of little watercolor-on-ivory plaques painted with flowers to "dealers" in the town of Épernay, just west of Äy on the river Marne.[1]

In 1876, the year his father died, René became an apprentice to the Parisian goldsmith

A rare enameled gold, ojime, and peridot necklace, circa 1890–95. The piece is important as an example of pure Japonisme in Lalique's work. Complete with original box. *Figure 1.*

Louis Aucoc. The apprenticeship was most likely urged by his mother, whose fatherless child was now compelled to leave his studies and devote his time and talents to practical career training, at least for a while. Lalique remained for two years with Aucoc, who was one of Paris's most successful, if traditional and largely unimaginative, jewelers, as indeed were most of the goldsmiths of the time, whose expensive, often diamond-laden pieces were, as one writer has noted, "wobbling wonders of intrinsic wealth . . . [which] ended up looking stiff and lifeless."[2] They were nothing at all like the dazzling Art Nouveau creations for which Lalique was to be praised extensively at the fin de siècle.

René went to London in 1878 for further study at what goldsmith and writer Henri Vever termed the "Collège de Sydenham," most likely the School of Art that had been established at the Crystal Palace, the massive glass-and-iron structure that was moved to Sydenham three years after its "unveiling" at the Great Exhibition of 1851. Sydenham was a suburb of south London where many French immigrants resided, so the young René may very well have lived with relatives or family friends there. Unfortunately, little is known of this two-year sojourn but that much of Lalique's study was devoted to drawing from nature and life. Art schools were considered more progressive and liberal in Britain than in France, and doubtless the predominant Arts and Crafts Movement, with its emphasis on virtuoso techniques and its love of nature, had an effect on the budding draftsman/goldsmith. The Sydenham school closed in 1880 and Lalique returned to Paris the same year, this time to study sculpture at the noted École Bernard Palissy, concurrently designing fabrics and wall coverings for a relative named Vuilleret.

A turning point of sorts occurred in Lalique's professional life in 1881, when he decided to try his luck as a free-lance jewelry designer. Louis Aucoc and Jules Destape as well as the firms of Boucheron and Cartier were among the Parisian *joailliers de luxe* who employed the talented young man. By 1885 Lalique was able to purchase an atelier of his own on the Place Gaillon (the premises of his former employer, Destape, who retired to Algeria soon afterward). With the opening of his own firm, Lalique began to make his name known (many of his free-lance pieces had been designed anonymously), and in no time his distinctive, nature-inspired designs were reproduced and hailed by critics and colleagues in the respected trade publication *Le Bijou*. His reputation and clientele grew, and his rightful place was taken at the crest of the *nouvelle vague* of the style called Art Nouveau.[3]

Today as in his own day, Lalique's jewelry is considered foremost among Art Nouveau goldwork, not only for its impeccable craftsmanship and strong nature-and-symbolist-oriented subject matter, but also for its innovative —indeed, revolutionary—combinations of materials and techniques. Unlike his immediate goldsmith predecessors—whose over-the-top, somewhat vulgar "masterpieces" were domi-

The only bronze statue known of René Lalique. Executed in bronze circa 1900–1910 by Théodore Rivière. Signed in the mold and with the inscription "à mon ami Lalique." *Figure 2.*

nated by large, showy diamonds in florid settings—Lalique created haunting, handsome pieces from a variety of ingredients. To be sure, he sometimes used diamonds, rubies, sapphires, and gold, but these in tandem with pearls, ivory, horn, and enamel, in configurations that ranged from the tenderest of neoclassical lovers, to the iciest of wintry landscapes, to the most numinous of hybrid human-insect creatures. These jewels included rings, bracelets, pendants, necklaces, and brooches, as well as haircombs, tiaras, and massive chest ornaments, some of these latter rather unwieldy, admittedly, and seldom, if ever, worn. His repertory of subjects was largely organic—floral, avian, serpentine, human—and he treated them dramatically, often with allegorical or symbolist overtones in the Art Nouveau manner. They were expertly executed in precious and semiprecious metals and stones, as well as in colored enamels and natural materials like ivory and tortoiseshell, by his crew of talented craftsmen, who interpreted Lalique's own detailed, meticulous, often annotated drawings and whose work was overseen by the master himself.

Lalique's clientele included many of Paris's leading lights—noted writers, performers, politicians, and businessmen, many of whom were his friends and who moved in the same upper-class, largely conservative circles as he did. His best-known customers were the great tragic actress Sarah Bernhardt (for whom he also designed stage pieces of costume jewelry—in effect, showy props) and the Armenian-born financier and petroleum magnate Calouste Gulbenkian, whose outstanding 150-piece collection of Lalique jewels (and some sculptures and glass) is today in the Lisbon museum bearing his name.

The jewels and other goldwork of René Lalique were some of the most admired creations of the Art Nouveau era—along with the glass of Émile Gallé and the furniture of Hector Guimard and Louis Majorelle—and they were also some of the most imitated works, albeit with a vast number of inferior products being the result. Such imitation did not at all flatter the *maître joaillier,* whose standards were the highest in his profession.

In time Lalique began to experiment with another material—glass—a medium that was to entrance him and eventually turn him away from goldwork altogether. Indeed, as early as the 1890s, some of Lalique's objects had been composed wholly or partially of glass. These were mostly works in *cire perdue,* or "lost wax," glass, a difficult technique adapted from bronze-casting and allowing only one "edition" per mold.

One no doubt partly embellished story dates to around 1893 and relates to Lalique's early experiments with glass and his future designs of flacons.

Throughout the past years, he had been seeking for a medium in which he could not only bring his art to its heights, but at the same time remove it from the luxury class, making it available to a wider public. Experimenting constantly, working feverishly, Lalique tried every medium which came to hand. Metals, shell, horn, various woods . . . he had used them all with conspicuous success. Still he was not satisfied.

Finally on one occasion he was executing a new design . . . a buckle of gold set with gemlike rock crystal. Here was the medium he sought . . . the material he knew so well, for had he not for years worked with enamels . . . glass transformed with oxides? Scientifically he knew the composition: sand, potash, lead . . . he understood it, he recognized its possibilities, he foresaw its artistic future in the hands of the master designer. In his own tiny kitchen he made his first experiment with pure glass . . . a tiny tear bottle, a droplike gem. It was molded

Probably the first perfume flacon by René Lalique in glass made by the *cire perdue* process in 1893. Exhibited at the Louvre, Paris, 1925–45. *Figure 3. EX-11*

in a simple cooking pan over the fire in his stove in Rue Thérèse. He piled on the wood, hotter grew the flame . . . in that fire not just a treasured work of art was formed, a great artistic idea was coming to life. In the intense heat, Lalique worked, alone, oblivious to his surroundings. Suddenly he became aware of crackling timber. His studio was afire, his experiment in danger. While his landlord rushed to put out the fire, Lalique saved his original experiment in glass.[4]

The chances are that the "tiny tear bottle," a 4-inch (10 cm)-long arrowhead-shaped *cire perdue* vial with stopper (Figure 3), molded on the inside with Oriental-looking fish, never held any scent, but its historical significance is great, one reason it was sold at auction at Phillips New York in 1980 for $37,000, then a near-record sum for Lalique glass.[5] Indeed, it was on exhibition at the Louvre, on loan from René Lalique, from 1925 to 1945, another indication of its prominent place in the master's *oeuvre.*

The Rue Thérèse address mentioned in the above account was in actuality Lalique's third atelier, the first being the studio at Place Gaillon and the second located on the Rue du Quatre-Septembre, its rental prompted by the inadequate space afforded by the former Destape atelier. The two workshops seem to have been in use concurrently until 1890, when Lalique acquired even larger premises at 20 Rue Thérèse. At the time his staff numbered around thirty, and the building on Rue Thérèse was spacious enough to accommodate his work force as well as provide a home (a third-story apartment) for himself and his wife. According to Lalique expert Félix Marcilhac, René Lalique was first married to Marie-Louise Lambert in 1886, who died at a young age. He was married a second time in 1902 to Augustine Ledru, daughter of the sculptor Auguste Ledru.[6]

3

4

A lovely portrait by Georges Clairin (1843–1919) inscribed "à mon ami Lalique" and signed by the artist. It is not clear whether the lady is René Lalique's first wife, Marie-Louise Lambert, who, according to Lalique expert Félix Marcilhac, he married in 1886 or his second wife, Augustine Ledru, daughter of the sculptor. The former is suggested by an exhibit label on the back of the portrait, indicating that it was shown at the Exposition Universelle in Paris in 1889. However, Georges Clairin was a good friend of Lalique and the Ledru family. Oil on canvas. *Figure 4.*

Although single-handed experiments in glass began in the last decade of the nineteenth century, Lalique's primary output until the early years of the present century was still goldwork —the aforementioned jewels as well as more ambitious objets d'arts, such as a silver, horn, and steel dagger depicting a battle scene, a full-length mirror with two bronze serpents serving as its striking frame, a silver and glass centerpiece in the shape of a lily pond laden with five nymphs, and even a quintet of patinated-bronze, wing- and web-sprouting female figures, which comprised an ornate grille "backdrop" for Lalique's jewelry display at the 1900 Exposition Universelle in Paris.

The 1900 Exposition marked a high point in terms of universal recognition of Lalique's genius as a goldsmith, but it also signaled the beginning of the decline of his output of jewelry, not in terms of quality but in regard to numbers.

A dazzling array of bejeweled and enameled pendants, buckles, bracelets, brooches, necklaces, hatpins, and haircombs dates from circa 1900–1905, but so too does an assortment of *cire perdue* glass pieces and, more importantly, toward the end of the first decade of the twentieth century, mass-produced glassworks, primarily perfume bottles.

In 1902, Lalique's work in glass moved from being a one-man endeavor to a group effort. For about a decade, a staff of four worked in a small atelier at a family estate in the village of Clairefontaine. Some of the architectural elements cast in glass were bound for yet another Lalique headquarters, an impressive seven-floor facility at 40 Cours la Reine (today known as Cours Albert 1ᵉʳ) that included workshops, a display area, and family living space. A retail shop was opened in 1905 at 24 Place Vendôme, a highly desirable address, which brought Lalique to the attention of a significant new clientele (not to mention neighboring merchant François Coty). In 1909 Lalique rented a glass factory at Combs-la-Ville, near Fontainebleau, largely due to his increased production of glass perfume bottles. He bought the glassworks within twelve months, and it flourished until World War I, at which time it was shut down, reopening in 1918. Production increased rapidly after the war, prompting the demand for even more space. This was filled by the construction of a new factory in Wingen-sur-Moder, in the old Alsace region.

In the 1920s and '30s, the output of Lalique et Cie was massive and clearly unsurpassed by that of any other similar fine art glass manufacturer in France. At the height of the interwar period the Lalique firm employed some 600 workers. Besides perfume bottles—which were created for fragrance companies' products as well as for retail sale—glass boxes, vases, mirrors, frames, seals, inkwells, paperweights, figural automobile mascots and other such statuettes, lighting devices, jewelry, and utilitarian tableware (tumblers, goblets, plates, trays, carafes, etc.) were produced in the tens of thousands.

Marc Lalique, René's only son (1900–1977),[7] managed the Wingen-sur-Moder factory from 1921 and succeeded his father as head and chief designer of the company after his father's death in 1945. He also oversaw the reopening of the Wingen factory, which had been damaged during the war. The Combs-la-Ville Glassworks operated during World War II, but since Wingen reopened, it has operated mainly as a support service and shipping facility. Marc was very much involved in marketing and technological aspects of the firm, although he later contributed designs as well, just as his daughter, Marie-Claude (born in 1935), does today.

Besides the glass objects mentioned above, Lalique designed an array of glass panels and even whole interior-design schemes, such as those for John Wanamaker's department store in Philadelphia, the Worth shop in Cannes, and Coty's Fifth Avenue showroom in New York. He produced tableware, lighting fixtures, and panels for the French ocean liner *Normandie,* the "Queen of the Seas," and he even redesigned the interior of a chapel on the isle of Jersey for the Boots family of the British drugstore chain, adorning altars, rails, windows, screens, and reredos with lovely stylized lilies.

The 1925 Exposition des Arts Décoratifs et Industriels Modernes in Paris proved the premier showcase for Lalique's Art Deco output, just as the 1900 Exposition Universelle had highlighted his Art Nouveau jewels. But Lalique's talent was even more evident at the later fair, which featured not only his small glass *objets d'art* in his own pavilion but also a massive outdoor fountain of his design that dazzled on the Esplanade des Invalides. He also made sizable contributions to the Sèvres and Parfumerie Française pavilions.

A previously unpublished photograph of the main Lalique gallery at 11 Rue Royale in Paris on the occasion of its opening in 1936. René Lalique's first retail outlet was at 24 Place Vendôme, where his creations were displayed for over thirty years prior to the 1936 move. The Rue Royale location remains the principal company retail outlet to this day. *Figure 5.*

After his triumph at the 1925 Exposition, the name Lalique spread across Europe, the United States, and South America, and his glass was purchased *en masse* by eager new customers. Breves Galleries in London sold his glassware, as did B. Altman and Saks Fifth Avenue in New York, Alexander and Oviatt in Los Angeles, and countless other fine retail establishments from St. Moritz to São Paulo. It is not within the purview of this volume to delve into aspects of Lalique's glass output other than his flacons, but it must be stressed again just how versatile this man was, how perspicacious, and how undeniably talented. Boxes, bowls, vases, chandeliers, statuettes; figurative, floral, geometric, abstract; crystal clear, milky opalescent, bold blue and red, sensuous amber and amethyst—the variety present throughout all his glass *oeuvre* is staggering. Lalique was a man to keep on top of the times as well—for example, designing an

5

assortment of human figures and animals intended to adorn the radiator caps and hoods of the still fairly new automobiles. One of these car mascots, *Victoire,* or *Spirit of the Wind* as it is often called (Figure 6), an androgynous head with long hair frozen behind in a stark geometric configuration, has become an icon of Art Deco and a symbol of speed. Electricity was still in its youth as well, and Lalique's array of lighting fixtures—floor-length, tabletop, pendent from the ceiling, wall sconce, etc.—display not only his design flair but his sensitivity to making an artificial light source appear not glaringly obvious but natural and beautiful.

In 1933, an exhibition of Lalique's glass was held at the Musée des Arts Décoratifs in Paris, an event unprecedented at the time for a living artist. And even in his later years, beset by debilitating arthritis, the *maître verrier* oversaw his massive and thriving business with the help of his son. His death in 1945 marked the end of an influential, enviable, and highly productive career—that of one of the past century's undeniably leading designers.

*V*ictoire, or *Spirit of the Wind,* is, no doubt, the most well known and dramatic of Lalique's car mascots *(bouchons de radiateur).* It was first produced about 1925 and is a wonderful symbol of the early adventuresome days of the automobile and of the Art Deco period. *Figure 6.*

CHAPTER 2

The Roots of the Perfume Industry

THE USE OF DISTINCTIVE AROMAS THAT ARE obtained naturally from flowers, herbs, roots, grasses, and even animals for a variety of purposes—whether that use be ritualistic, religious, cosmetic, or curative—has existed for millennia. Egyptian papyri and wall paintings describe and depict exotic aromatics used to perfume the air as well as various parts of the body, both male and female, living or dead; Hindus have long offered sacrifices to their deity Attar in temples built of innately fragrant woods; pleasurable scents are alluded to often in the Old and New Testaments (notably frankincense, or olibanum, and myrrh); Murasaki Shikibu, in the eleventh-century Japanese classic *The Tale of Genji,* mentions a guessing game whose noble players attempt to identify a scent; and even the prophet Mohammed's often-harsh words sing the praises of sweet floral extracts, especially camphire, an archaic name for henna. Indeed, myriad writers of history, poetry, and drama alike, from Homer, Pliny, and Plutarch to T'ang Dynasty poet Li Po, Shakespeare, and Baudelaire, refer in one way or another to the power, glory, beauty, and sometimes even folly and evil of scents.

An experimental Lalique design of significant interest, since it copies a production vase. The miniature flacon version is clear with a plain disk stopper. The vase is shown in Figure 8. Probably 1910s. *Figure 7. EX-2*

Spice-derived perfumes—especially in the guise of burning incense (the word *perfume* comes from the Latin *per* and *fumar,* literally, "thoroughly to smoke")—were among the first used in early ancient and later biblical times. Doctors prescribed perfumes for assorted ailments, priests concocted supreme essences to be offered to various deities, and the hygiene-conscious Egyptians applied perfumed oils to their bodies after formal bathing, as the biblical heroines Esther and Judith did, the former to ritually purify herself, the latter to tempt Holofernes. Wood and floral aromas soon abounded, and in Pharaonic Egypt a hybrid essence called *kyphi* was extremely popular. Among the scent's sixteen ingredients were aspalathus, cardamom, cypress, dock, honey, juniper, myrrh, raisins, and saffron, which resulted, no doubt, in a heady, delectable, almost comestible product.

Arabia supplied most of the essences used in the ancient world. Around A.D. 900 an Arabian physician, Avicenna, was probably the first to use distillation to extract volatile oils from flowers, fragrant rose water being one of his creations.

The eagles design at the neck and base of this substantial production vase is the model for the experimental scent bottle shown in Figure 7. *Figure 8.*

Early Egyptian perfume containers have survived and, interestingly, although some are of carved calcite (similar to alabaster) and onyx, most are made of opaque glass, such as a turquoise flacon bearing the name of Queen Hatshepsut dating to Dynasty XVIII (1500 B.C.). They were largely made by wrapping molten glass around a core of sand, and most come from the delta of the Nile and from Tyre and Sidon on the shores of Phoenicia. The Phoenicians' bottles, in shades of green, blue, purple, and yellow, much like their Egyptian counterparts, were sometimes decorated while hot with wavy, striped threads, or combed patterns, often even with thin lines of gold leaf. In Sidon, at the end of the first century B.C., the method of blowing glass was invented.

The classical Romans produced large amounts of glass, and their flacons were generally of translucent, crystal, or semicrystal glass, with globular bodies and long necks terminating in wide rims. The beginnings of the Christian era witnessed a waning of interest in perfume in Europe, although spices, usually in incense form, were used in religious ceremonies (akin to the Three Magi's offerings of aromatic gum resins frankincense and myrrh to the infant Jesus). The vessels containing these scents and oils were largely of plain and undecorated glass, although some etched, gold-leafed examples are known. After the fall of Rome, glass continued to flourish in Muslim Egypt and in other parts of the Middle East, and molten-glass bottles, some with cut or engraved decoration, survive today.

With the onset of the Crusades—and the return of the Crusaders to the West from the mysterious East—a revival of interest in scents took place. By the twelfth century, the precursors of modern *parfumeurs* appear in the annals of history. In England, the Guild of Pepperers in London, mentioned as early as 1179, comprised merchants who sold drugs and spices obtained from Red Sea ports and locations further east. The Guild of Apothecaries took over the trade from the spicers in later years, although chemists and even alchemists played important roles in developing scents, such as the aromatic waters of rosemary and lavender. Perfumes were highly popular in Tudor England, though most of these were imported from Italy and France. One of the earliest mentions of a perfumer in London is on a trade card from the late seventeenth or early eighteenth century, now in the British Museum, advertising one "Charles Lilie, Perfumer," who had a shop "at the Corner of Beaufort-Buildings in the Strand" where he concocted and sold snuffs, perfumed waters, soaps, and various other items "which refresh the brain in those that have too much for their quiet, and gladdens [*sic*] it in those who have too little to know the want of it."[1]

In Italy the allure of perfume first made itself felt in the early 1500s in Venice, which was an important center of commerce, with merchant ships arriving from Constantinople and points east. Domestic scents were first cultivated there by monks, who were often tenders of rich gardens and knowledgeable of the necessary sciences of chemistry and botany as well. In 1508, the Dominicans in Florence's monastery of Santa Maria Novella set up a laboratory for the processing of both aromatic scents and therapeutic elixirs. In the seventeenth and eighteenth centuries, this laboratory was renowned for its perfumes, which, according to one writer, "were placed in tiny bottles in small boxes or cases, often in the shape of a book, the cover being stamped with ornamental devices in gold or colour."[2] In the fifteenth century in Rome, the essence known today as frangipani was devised, supposedly by a member of the noble Roman family, the Frangipanis. At first made in the form of a dry powder, it later appeared in a liquid state, probably thanks to Mercutio Frangipani, who distilled the powder in wine, thereby creating a longer-lasting scent. The fragrance was derived from sweet-smelling tropical American shrubs of the *Plumeria* genus, *P. rubra* and *P. alba*. (Mercutio was said to have become acquainted with the scent on a West Indies voyage with none other than Christopher Columbus.)[3]

The containers for Italian scents, indeed for most European-made fragrances, were largely of Venetian glass from the famous island center of Murano. Elegant colorless, tinted, and decorated glass was produced in great quantity, the latter including *millefiori* (literally, *a thousand flowers*) glass, which is comprised of rods of colored glass carefully fused together and then polished to give the effect of myriad tiny blossoms. Florentine glassmakers also created exquisite per-

Unique square section flacon with fish heads at four corners. Experimental design with plain stopper.
Figure 9. EX-3

fume bottles, usually of cut crystal. Such flacons were introduced to France by Catherine de' Medici, wife of the French king Henry II, although the monarch set up a glassworks at Saint-Germain-en-Laye, where he hired two Italian masters to create stunning pieces for the ladies of his court, including Diane de Poitiers.

The making and selling of perfume in France was an important trade by the reign of Henry II (1519–59), whose aforementioned consort, Catherine de' Medici, brought her own perfumer with her from Italy, one René le Florentin, in addition to Cosmo Ruggiero, her personal astrologer and alchemist, who also concocted perfumes for his mistress. René was soon to open a fancy shop in the Pont au Change in Paris (where he also sold poisons!), which was supposedly a popular meeting place for late-sixteenth-century Parisian glitterati. Paris records mention native *parfumeurs* as early as the twelfth century. Near the start of his 1180–1223 reign, Philippe-Auguste (Philip II) passed a law that in effect established the first guild of French *parfumeurs*. But it was not until the seventeenth century, under Jean-Baptiste Colbert, chief minister of Louis XIV, that the *parfumeurs* were able to obtain patents, which were duly registered in Parliament.

Colbert was a great patron of the Norman glassmakers, and he supported as well Italian-born Bernard Perrot (né Bernardo Perrotto) of Orléans, among whose creations is attributed a body of scent bottles, usually brown or blue with fleur-de-lis and heart-shaped blossoms relief-molded on pear-shaped flattened bodies. Other glass bottles in eighteenth-century France include similarly shaped examples depicting figures, coats-of-arms, and other subjects in tiny *verre-églomisé* beads that have been applied to an ivory or glass ground. The Venetian technique of *millefiori* glass was adopted by the Baccarat factory among other French glassworks near Lunéville in the northeastern part of France, and this still-existent firm produced scent bottles with this decoration.

By the eighteenth century, perfume was a major "industry" in France, and glassmakers, as well as goldsmiths and assorted craftsmen who produced stunningly embellished scent bottles, were kept quite busy with scent-related commissions.

Louis XIV, the Sun King, had a perfumer named Martial whom he used to receive in his private quarters, although he supposedly frowned upon the excessive use of scent in his court. The court of his successor, Louis XV, which was sometimes referred to as *la cour parfumée* (the perfumed court), represented perhaps the apogee of perfumed France, and its members were said to have sported a different scent every day, sometimes even several a day (this likely because of the custom of infrequent bathing). Madame de Pompadour, Louis's titled mistress and the foremost tastemaker of the day, was supposed to have spent something in the region of 500,000 livres in one year on fragrances at Choisy-le-Roi—and one can only guess at the large amount she must have parted with for the elaborate glass, gold, silver, porcelain, and other bottles in which she kept her precious scents, two of which were *eau de Portugal* and *huile de Venus*. Another of Louis's partners, Madame du Barry, started a fashion for eau de cologne in France as well, one which would continue unabated for decades. Indeed, art historian Kate Foster has termed the 1700s "the most fruitful period in the history of the scent bottle,"[4] which is in part confirmed by the fact that some names

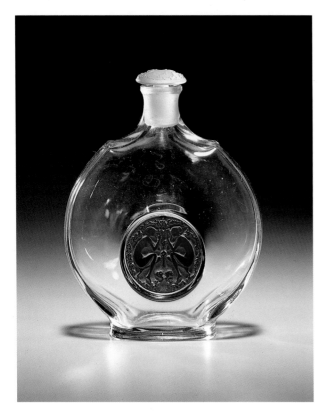

Early circular flask with amber inset of two nudes. Experimental/unique.
Figure 10. EX-4

10

with which we are quite familiar today—Houbigant and Roger et Gallet, for instance, both of which commissioned Lalique to design bottles for them—date from the eighteenth or early nineteenth century. In England and America, too, still-existent perfumers started out in the 1700s, including Woods of Windsor, Floris, and Yardley in Britain, and Caswell-Massey in Newport, Rhode Island.

The perfumes being produced during this fertile period include, among other floral essences, violet and rose—apparent favorites of Marie Antoinette, the queen of Louis XVI. Patrick Süskind, in his riveting 1985 novel, *Perfume* (subtitled *The Story of a Murderer*), about a man with the greatest sense of smell in France but possessing no actual scent himself, describes the character Grenouille's first encounter with perfume in 1750s Paris, having been exposed beforehand only to base, ordinary smells:

> It was here [in the Faubourg Saint-Germain area] as well that Grenouille first smelled perfume in the literal sense of the word: a simple lavender or rose water, with which the fountains of the gardens were filled on gala occasions; but also the more complex, more costly scents, of tincture of musk mixed with oils of neroli and tuberose, jonquil, jasmine, or cinnamon, that floated behind the carriages like rich ribbons on the evening breeze. . . .
>
> He knew many of these ingredients already from the flowers and spice stalls at the market; others were new to him, and he filtered them out from the aromatic mixture and kept them unnamed in his memory: ambergris, civet, patchouli, sandalwood, bergamot, vetiver, opopanax, benzoin, hop blossom, castor. . . .[5]

Indeed, flowers were now being grown aplenty in the sunbaked hilly Var region of southeast France for the express purpose of extracting their scents, as they are still grown in profusion today (despite the artificial ingredients making up so many scents). In the eighteenth and nineteenth centuries, the area from Grasse to Nice must have been one big flower garden: roses, tuberoses, jasmine, and the acacia called cassie around Cannes; violets from Nice; lavender, rosemary, and thyme from Nîmes; and carnations from the Italian Riviera. All these and more flowers provided the scents of the French beau monde, not to mention hyacinths from Holland and lavender from England. But besides pure floral scents, scented bouquets—that is, multi-ingredient fragrances—were popular in eighteenth-century France—for instance, the heady essence of chypre (from the French for Cyprus, where it may have originated), still a favorite today. Early recipes for chypre differed, but among its essential ingredients were usually

A square flask, probably experimental, with sunburst/floral design from concave center. Stopper is from commercial stock (*Jamerose*, de Vigny—Figure 199). Also see Figure 88 for examples with the same motif. *Figure 11.* EX-6

oakmoss, musk, ambergris, sandalwood, orris, and rose. Men's fragrances became popular, even more so in the next century, when Napoleon Bonaparte was said to have emptied "two quarts of eau de Cologne a week and sixty flasks of Spanish jasmine essence a month."[6]

His wife, Empress Josephine, favored musk, civet, and other rich, heady scents, and period sources mention their overpowering presence in her dressing room—which her husband apparently found objectionable—as well as their long-lasting aromas, present at her Malmaison apartments for some time after her demise.

An important character in the cast of French *parfumeurs* at the time was a gentleman who founded a firm later connected to Lalique and still in existence today. The *marchand-parfumeur* Jean-François Houbigant (1752–1807) opened his Paris shop on the then-new and still fashionable Rue du Faubourg Saint-Honoré, number 19, in 1775, embellishing it with a sign reading: À LA CORBEILLE DE FLEURS (AT THE SIGN OF THE BASKET OF FLOWERS). Besides creating perfumes, powders, and pomades, he also advertised himself as a purveyor of then-modish scented gloves and of *le véritable rouge végétal* (authentic vegetable rouge). Among Houbigant's best-selling scents were *eau de lys* and *eau de bergamotte,* and his estimable clients included Marie Antoinette (who supposedly was having an order filled for her at Houbigant's shop on the night of her escape to Varennes!). Houbigant and his contemporaries were only slightly affected by the French Revolution, and soon afterward, in the days of the Muscadins, the Incroyables, and the Merveilleuses, they thrived once more. In 1900, Fernand Javal of the House of Houbigant created Idéal, the first composite perfume, and in 1913 Quelques Fleurs, the first floral bouquet ever and still a success today, was launched. Lalique's connection with the House of Houbigant included designing bottles for their scents La

Belle Saison, Le Temps de Lilas, and Chypre.

Another significant personage in early French *parfumerie* was Jean-Marie Farina, the inventor of eau de cologne, whose firm was taken over much later by Roger et Gallet in 1862. Born Johann Maria Farina in Cologne in 1685, he began producing and selling *aqua mirabilis,* or *Wunderwasser.* At first promoted for its medicinal qualities (it was mixed with water, wine, and other liquids and drunk as a preventive or curative elixir), by the end of the eighteenth century its appeal as a freshener grew. The liquid itself was more or less identical to citrus fragrances developed much earlier in Italian monasteries, but it took a German to give the product a French name, possibly as a result of its use by French soldiers during the Seven Years' War of 1756–63. When Johann Maria Farina died a rich and successful businessman in 1766, the firm passed to his nephew of the same name, but by then competitors reared their ugly heads throughout Germany, using the same name and flooding the marketplace with Johann Maria Farina, or Jean-Marie Farina, eau de cologne. Farina's eau de cologne, as well as that of a late-eighteenth-century rival, Ferdinand Muhlens's *4711,* are still produced today and are considered classics.

The perfume bottles of eighteenth- and nineteenth-century Europe display a range of mediums, shapes, motifs, and sizes. There were pomanders of various forms—bells, heads, animals—which were small portable openwork containers intended to hold solid fragrances pulverized into a globular shape. The smelling box, a closed container for solid or dry perfume, became extremely popular by the eighteenth century; however, these were generally of base metal. *Brûle-parfums,* perfume lamps or incense burners, made out of glass, stoneware, and a variety of materials and many in complex figural or animal shapes, were also used.

But glass was by far the predominant material used to contain perfumes in the seventeenth, eighteenth, and nineteenth centuries, and, as direct application of a liquid scent to the body superseded other indirect perfuming methods, so the scent bottle took over as the most prevalent way of storing scents. Of course, the perfume bottle was considered decorative as well as utilitarian, and it is safe to assume that every bottle in madame's collection did not necessarily contain a scent (as the vintage examples do not today). Indeed, the decorative bottles were purchased separately from the scents, the fragrances themselves usually being packaged in plain glass vials such as pharmacists used for medicines. By the late seventeenth century, perfume began to be used by the bourgeoisie in addition to the nobility, necessitating greater production of cheaper decorative scent bottles. This demand was filled by Perrot and other French glassmakers, who produced largely mold-blown glass (and later pressed glass), as opposed to cut glass.

For example, some lovely colored-glass bottles were made between 1830 and 1840 by Launey Hautin & Cie, a Parisian firm. Thick walled and usually of a deep-hued red, the bottles were adorned with relief designs, many mimicking those of architecture of the time: rococo scrolls, Gothic Revival arches, trefoils, etc. Other glass bottles were of simple blown forms—some round and flattened, others long and narrow—and were cold-painted with floral and genre scenes, usually in Germany and Bohemia, up until the nineteenth century.

Bottles from England, Ireland, Germany, and eastern and southern Europe proliferated throughout all of Europe, finding their way to France. Glass scent bottle production was at its peak in the early-nineteenth-century Empire and Biedermeier periods, when, as Edmund Launert put it, besides coloring being used on a large scale, virtually "every single piece was also elaborately cut or, to a lesser extent, engraved."[7] Color also had a practical advantage over colorless glass, in that light hastens the deterioration of a scent. This is not the case today, since chemical preservatives are added to perfumes to extend their lives.

Metallic elements were added to glass to produce colors such as red (from copper or sometimes even gold), blue (cobalt or copper oxide), green (chromium oxide), yellow (cadmium sulfide, silver chloride, or antimony), or purple (manganese). Pearly white opaline or opalescent glass was common as well, and continued to be so into the early twentieth century, when Lalique strongly guarded the formula for his stunning semitranslucent opalescent glass (not generally used for his flacons). The term *opaline* was first used in 1820 by the Baccarat glassworks, although glass vessels of this basic type had been made by Perrot in Orléans in the late seventeenth century. By the early nineteenth century, Bohemian factories manufactured huge

13

amounts of opalescent glass and French glass-works followed suit, producing arguably the handsomest examples of such scent bottles, often embellished with silver or gilt floral motifs.

Other means of surface-coloring and decorating glass in the eighteenth and nineteenth centuries included overlay, staining, and flashing, the latter, most common, method consisting of dunking the clear-glass bulb into molten colored glass and then rapidly withdrawing it. The gaffer would then reheat the whole piece and make it into the desired shape. The resultant colored surface is rather thin, but colorful nonetheless. The traditional Italian methods of coloring glass, the *latticino* (the inclusion of white glass threads) and *millefiori* (colored rods) techniques, were applied in other countries as well. *Latticino* (from the Italian word for milk) glass soon was not restricted to white alone, the German glassworks widening the repertory to include other hues and the French, at Clichy and Choisy-le-Roi, going one step further and including different colored threads in a complex zigzag pattern. The thriving tourist trade in Venice meant that such bottles found their way into collections all over Europe, as well as the New World, and were imitated in nearly as many places.

By the end of the Victorian era and at the dawning of the new century, scent bottles had become commonplace in the boudoirs of all but the lowest classes. Cased and carved cameo glass bottles were first made in Britain—some directly influenced by Chinese snuff bottles—and such oddities as two-opening double-scent bottles were briefly in vogue. On the whole, though, the quality of scent bottles—and indeed of much glass of the Victorian era in France, Britain, and elsewhere—had sharply decreased, concurrent with its growing production. Scent bottles of even more outlandish shapes and designs were made, such as miniature pistols and champagne bottles, and manufacturers fell back on the past

An important large decanterlike eau de toilette. Experimental/unique, circa 1910. Mask of female on either side of modified baluster form. *Figure 13.* EX-10

by making examples reminiscent of eighteenth-century or even earlier creations. Tiny pocket flacons of glass were encased in filigreed silver worked in dazzling lacy configurations, but the inner material was secondary to the outer covering.

The glass bottles that brought France to the fore again at the turn of the century, after languishing for some time in unimaginative, repetitive historicization, were those created in the exuberant Art Nouveau style. Émile Gallé of Nancy and his contemporaries, the brothers Antonin and Auguste Daum, Eugène Rousseau, American Louis Comfort Tiffany, and the Austrian firm J. & L. Lobmeyr, produced exquisite scent bottles that displayed the new curvilinear, nature-inspired style that was a direct reaction against previous stilted ones. Gallé's rare and stunning flacons were of overlaid cut glass, the inner layer usually a lighter shade than the dramatic outer one, which often sported florid and/or leafy silhouettes, all amazingly close to nature.

Tiffany, a goldsmith and glassmaker like Lalique but working in the Art Nouveau period only, created precious jewels of scent bottles, including one outstanding round example, its overlaid glass body in the form of a bursting mauve chrysanthemum, its somewhat imposing gold top a two-headed lion terminating at the bottle's neck in a giant paw. It is akin to Chinese snuff bottles and is neoclassical, a floral and faunal hybrid creature that was quite unlike anything else being made at the time. Other, simpler examples were tiny, organic-shaped bottles of Tiffany's iridescent Favrile glass, with metal stoppers and mounts; these were intended to be kept in a purse and could not be stood up and displayed.

René Lalique was an early participant in this movement and at the turn of the century designed several unique scent bottles as a goldsmith before embarking on his long career in glass.

The Birth of Lalique Perfume Bottles

DESPITE THE HIGHLY EMBELLISHED STORY OF THE creation of Lalique's first glass perfume bottle, related in the first chapter, this trail-blazing experience did not lead to immediate mass production of glass flacons. Indeed, that did not occur until a decade or so later, following the most auspicious meeting of Lalique and François Coty. Before turning to the early years of the twentieth century, however, we must mention several of Lalique's lovely bejeweled objects of the late 1890s, namely some perfume bottle designs, two of which are in the Musée des Arts Décoratifs in Paris and are included in Sigrid Barten's *René Lalique: Schmuck und Objets d'Arts 1890–1910.*[1]

One of the Paris bottles, which was given to the museum by Lalique himself in 1896, is 1¾ inches (4.2 cm) high and depicts a burst of enameled amethyst stars (looking more like highly irregular inkblots) on a rock-crystal ground; it is capped by a precious metal stopper embedded with five cabochon garnets (Figure 14). The interesting abstract astral design has no precedents in Lalique's goldwork, although a field of stars served as background for a bevy of black velvet

An elaborate, very early model, no doubt made for a jewelry client. *Amethyst.* Experimental/unique. Rock crystal, enamel, silver, and amethyst. 1896. *Figure 14.* EX-9

bats on a gray gauze canopy overhanging Lalique's jewelry display at the 1900 Paris Exposition, and the same bat-and-star design decorates an enameled copper, opal, and brilliant ankle bracelet of 1902–1906. Stars did play a role in Lalique's later works in glass, however: the wide borders of a rectangular mirror/picture frame, *Étoiles* (see 1932 catalog, plate 66, number 259), feature myriad five-pointed stars of many sizes. And of course there is Lalique's well-known perfume bottle design for Worth's *Dans la Nuit* scent, a sphere depicting a galaxy of bas-relief five-pointed stars, some in clear crystal on a nocturnal blue ground, others against a clear glass sky (Figure 15). The rock-crystal, gold, and gem-studded Paris bottle, however, is a unique piece in Lalique's goldsmith output as well as in his entire design repertory. Not so the other Musée des Arts Décoratifs flacon, a 2½-inch (6.1-cm)-high unsigned bottle. The red-black agate body is entwined by a silver serpent, whose head and neck serve as the stopper (Figure 16). A gift of Henri Vever to the museum in 1924, the flacon dates from around 1898–99 and is one of many serpentine subjects Lalique de-

15

picted, the best known perhaps being his circa 1924 *Serpent* vase (see 1932 catalog, plate 1, number 896) in colored glass, whose coiling body wholly comprises the globular vessel. Lalique's works in precious and nonprecious metal often depict snakes—a popular Art Nouveau theme because of its innate curvilinearity.

A snake also appeared on the scent bottle *Serpent* (Figure 40), whose open-jawed head was the stopper and whose often brown-stained body curved around the bottle's ovoid form. This bottle is a direct descendant of the silver and agate flacon, especially in terms of their similarly fashioned stoppers. A twisting mass of snakes also decorated a Lalique glass inkwell (see 1932 catalog, plate 74, number 432) of flattened circular shape.

Sigrid Barten includes other early Lalique perfume bottle designs in her volume, including the horn and rock-crystal *Thistle Blossom* flacon in the Staatliche Museen, Berlin; an unusual snail-shell, gilt-silver, and amethyst example in the collection of a Paris art dealer, Nourhan Manoukian; and several interesting drawings— pen, pencil, and/or colored wash on paper—for bottles featuring a leaf design, two with elaborate multicabochon stoppers (topping plain bottles), two with floral design (lotus blossom and poppy), and another with an avian motif. Unfortunately, none of these bottles is known to exist. Nonetheless, a perusal of Sigrid Barten's exhaustive book—specifically pages 536–38, catalog numbers 1674–84—is a worthwhile exercise for anyone wanting a more complete picture of Lalique's earliest work in perfume bottle design.

The era just following the successful 1900 Paris Exposition, where Lalique experienced a triumph, was the dawning of a brand-new century, and not only did the glass industry find itself becoming more and more mechanized and able to produce better-quality goods in ever-

Left: The small version of the cobalt blue flask for *Dans la Nuit*. 1920s. Left: The well-known Worth globe with blue enamel and molded stars for *Dans la Nuit*. Many sizes. Also made until the 1950s without "R." in signature. Reintroduced 1985 molded "Creation Lalique." Figure 15. W-2, W-104, W-1, W-103

increasing numbers, but also makers of scents could create high-quality perfumes at relatively cheap prices. Recent chemical discoveries— namely, artificial imitations of the costly essences heretofore crucial in creating good scents—made for an ever-wider palette from which more and more perfumers could create a plethora of perfumes. *Parfumeurs* were constantly realizing new scents. Amazingly, it was, as expert Nicholas M. Dawes has written, still "common for individual druggists to concoct their own scents and eau de colognes, offering them for sale in plain glass pharmaceutical bottles wrapped in waxed

17

The superb *Silver Serpent*, made during Lalique's jewelry years. Experimental/ unique. Agate and silver. 1898–99. Figure 16. EX-8

paper."[2] The alternatives were very costly hand-made bottles available to the upper classes or else cheap containers that badly imitated the real thing or were simply badly designed and made. There was doubtless a void to be filled by those with the right knowledge and facilities.

It was into this heady atmosphere of fervent productivity, relatively inexpensive materials, and packaging that was too dear or too plain or too unattractive that François Coty and René Lalique came. Together they made Coty's prediction that he would manufacture the finest perfume, present it in a simple but elegant container, and offer it to the consumer at a reasonable price[3]—but still as an *objet de luxe*—come phenomenally and profitably true.

In 1904 the House of Coty—La Maison de Coty—was founded in Paris by François Coty (1874–1934). It is the ultimate testimony to this far-seeing *parfumeur* nonpareil that to this day, nearly a century later, his name is still one of the best known in the world of fragrance. The long-lasting working relationship between Coty and René Lalique was the most successful of Lalique's profitable partnerships with perfume makers; it was not only Lalique's first such union, but the fruits of the collaboration—though not as numerous as those done for Worth or D'Orsay—were arguably the most sophisticated and original of Lalique's scent bottle designs and today rank with collectors among his rarest and most valuable.

The middle-class, well-educated Coty—born Francisco Giuseppe Spoturno in Ajaccio, Corsica—began his career as assistant to a French political and literary figure. But soon the young man abandoned this position and turned his attention to the retail trade, first selling point lace, then perfume. The catalyst for the change was Coty's friendship with a chemist, Raymond Goery, a man whose pastimes included concocting scents that he offered for sale in his apothe-

A pair of oil paintings by an anonymous French artist. The right panel illustrates the L. T. Piver shop on the Rue Royale next to the Madeleine and the other scene depicts perfume flacons in the window of the shop at the corner of the Place Vendôme and the Rue de la Paix in Paris. The latter is the exact location of Coty's first outlet. Probably these were done in a perfume-related exhibition and possibly there were four to six panels in all. *Figure 17.*

cary shop. Like many of these small-scale *parfumeurs*, the chemist sold his eau de cologne in inexpensively produced glass pharmaceutical bottles without labels or any type of packaging, except perhaps the aforementioned waxed-paper wrapping. It was Goery who suggested his friend visit the perfume distilleries at Grasse, which he did, and it was soon afterward that he borrowed enough money to move to Paris.

Coty became intrigued with the whole concept and business of fragrance, and he soon envisioned a totally new method of marketing desirable scents. Not only did Coty possess a keen business sense and a mind swimming with revolutionary ideas about perfume, but he also found he had "a great nose"—that extraordinary, almost superhuman sense of smell that, for the French, is a prerequisite for any *parfumeur*. Coty considered fragrance an *objet de luxe*, a thing of beauty, and he wanted the packaging of outstanding perfume to reflect this belief with stunning (but not vulgar) flacons, with engraved, even gilded labels, with leather and wooden boxes lined with silk, and so on. But his perfume would not be aimed at only the richest *parisiennes.*

So, with the financial backing and obvious trust and confidence of several firms that produced the essential oils used in creating perfume, Coty set up a business residence at 61 Rue la Boétie. The mostly floral scents he began to develop were to become the rage of Europe's beau monde. One legendary story related by the Coty firm today tells of the unique manner in which Coty's nascent product came to be sold in Paris's finest *grands magasins,* or department stores.[4] La Rose Jacqueminot—named after a popular cabbage-rose variety of the time, itself named after a French general—was offered to the Louvre department store by Coty, but the *parfumeur*'s product was roundly dismissed by the buyer until Coty just happened to drop the bottle onto

the floor, shattering it to pieces, but allowing the seductive scent to waft over the selling floor. Almost immediately women within reach of the fragrance demanded to know what the scent was and where they could buy it. Thus, La Rose Jacqueminot came to be stocked at all the *de luxe* Parisian stores.

The self-confident and perhaps more than slightly arrogant Coty had predicted, as mentioned previously, that he would make the finest scent, present it in a tasteful container, sell it reasonably, and thereby bring the world of commerce to its feet. If he was to fulfill his prophecy, he needed to discover a more economical way to mass-produce the bottles for his fragrances. He had been using Baccarat's glass-making factory for this purpose at a relatively expensive price before the opportune arrival of Lalique on the scene.

By 1906, the two gentlemen had nearby business addresses on Paris's fashionable Place Vendôme, Lalique at number 24, Coty at number 23. An elegant, anonymous painting of the time (Figure 17) represents Coty's shop on the Place Vendôme on the left, complete with handsome window display and a parade of modishly attired lady shoppers with their parasols, no doubt some of them customers at one or both of the men's shops.

Coty asked his neighbor to design labels first, then scent bottles, for his House of Coty. The exact date and circumstances of the first meeting of these two remarkable men are not known, but according to Georges Vindry of the Musée Internationale de la Parfumerie in Grasse, it was François Carnot, once president of the Union Centrale des Arts Décoratifs, an influential group founded in the late 1800s to promote the industrial arts reform movement, who introduced Coty to Lalique.[5] Carnot, who created the perfume section at the 1900 Exposition Universelle and later, in 1918, helped set up the Musée

19

The standard *Série Toilette* bottle for Coty that was used for many Coty scents. Briar design on stopper. Circa 1909. *Figure 18. C-12*

de Grasse, no doubt knew both men from the fair, if not earlier. Carnot as go-between makes perfect sense, although his name is not mentioned in Gabriel Mourey's rather romantic rendering of the initial circumstances leading to Coty's commissioning Lalique to design his bottles.

> With the exception of Gallé, very few [glass] artists had seen the part which could be played both industrially and artistically by this admirable material. But Lalique's fertile imagination saw all its decorative possibilities . . . to infinity. Was it not then a case of building up everything again—or rebuilding? He was in this state of mind when he was visited by the parfumeur,

Coty, who came to ask him to make glass [*sic*] labels for the scent-bottles manufactured by Cristalleries de Baccarat. First of all, Lalique refused. To design the whole bottle might interest him, but to add a decorative motive to an already existing bottle seemed to him puerile and supererogatory. If M. Coty would leave him free to do what he liked, he, Lalique, would be satisfied. So M. Coty gave in. . . . [Lalique] was enamored of the idea of making the scent-bottle a work of art, a precious vessel containing a precious essence.[6]

Coty's popular scents and business acumen combined with Lalique's artistic sensibility and technical skill resulted in a final product that brought the clients to the shops selling Coty fragrances—and, yes, the world of commerce to its feet.

The first bottles designed by Lalique for Coty were produced at the glassworks of Legras and Company, the large firm in St. Denis, near Paris, that had been founded in 1864. The bottles were unsigned, relatively simple rectangular or square flasks, but with decorative stoppers and handsome labels designed by Lalique. By 1910, Coty's bottles were being made at Lalique's Combs-la-Ville factory; these later bottles, as Nicholas M. Dawes has observed,[7] were made of *demi-cristal* glass, glass with a lower lead content and consequently "warmer" and "softer" than Legras's crisper, cleaner *cristal* products (12 percent as opposed to 24 percent lead content). They were easier and cheaper to manufacture, though no less beautiful—characteristics that doubtless appealed to Coty the businessman.

In all, Lalique designed at least sixteen bottles and labels for his friend Coty, who in the 1920s had become one of France's wealthiest men, obtaining control of the conservative daily *Le Figaro* in the early 1920s and founding in subsequent years two other right-wing, anti-

communist, and antisocialist papers largely subsidized by the profits from his fragrance empire. Coty also put together a collection of paintings and objets d'art of considerable significance, and he was a member of the Corsican senate. No doubt Coty's healthy resources were of great assistance to Lalique, especially during the earlier part of his glass-making career.[8]

The variety of bottles, stoppers, boxes, testers, promotional pieces, labels, even signs designed by Lalique for Coty from 1907 through at least the early 1930s (Coty died in 1934) could comprise a book of their own. Although not all

Promotional items by René Lalique for Coty, probably circa 1910. A bronze plaque used as a shop display piece, along with a tester for various Coty perfumes in a fitted box that includes a miniature of the plaque on the back panel. Three known. The plaque design was used in many other Coty promotional and packaging items. *Figure 19.*

of Coty's fragrances were bottled in Lalique creations, most of them were, and sometimes different perfumes were sold in the same bottle, with the same stoppers, though with different labels—making for considerable confusion among collectors today, especially when the original label is no longer affixed to the glass.[9] One rectangular section bottle, for instance (Figure 18, known as *Série Toilette,* or *Briar,* from the motif on its stopper), dating from circa 1908–1909 and bearing various Lalique signatures, was used for at least twelve scents: La Rose Jacqueminot, Ambre Antique, Émeraude, Jasmin de

glass store display sign by Lalique for Coty. The letters are recessed and frosted, the face is green enamel. Molded "R. Lalique." Probably 1910s. *Figure 20.*

Corse, L'Effleurt, La Jacée, L'Aimant, Chypre, Styx, L'Or, Muguet, and L'Origan.[10]

One of the most interesting of the containers designed by Lalique for Coty, probably before 1910, was a wooden box, which had space for a dozen tester bottles. The gilt-metal bas-relief plaque affixed to the inside top of the box is a florid representation of three cavorting female nudes, over whose heads waft the highly stylized words "Les Parfums de Coty" (see Figure 19 for the tester box as well as a large version of the bronze plaque that was used as a store display sign; Figure 20 shows an additional Coty shop sign in green enamel on glass. Both are signed "R. Lalique").

The labels and signs designed by Lalique for Coty were often gilded with thick, dense, curvilinear lettering in the Art Nouveau mode (the Art Deco style, with its geometric, rectilinear bent, was still at least a decade away). Some featured flowers that figured in their name (or in the scent itself), a few depicted languorous nudes. Labels did not come attached to every Coty bottle, however; some flacons had their scent's

names molded in relief directly on them as well as the name Coty.

The Coty bottles and Lalique's Maison Lalique glass flacons are the most significant within the entire massive *oeuvre*, the relatively small selection of Coty's bottles because of its initial place in the roster of commercial bottles Lalique created, the larger assortment of Maison Lalique flacons because of its direct connection to the man (he designed, created, and sold them, either through his own shop or through other retailers). In essence, the Maison Lalique scent bottles form the sturdy foundation of Lalique's entire perfume bottle output (many of his commercial perfume bottles relate to these designs), while the flacons for Coty are the mortar that enabled the other building materials—the bottles subse-

L'Effleurt de Coty was probably the first Lalique bottle for Coty, circa 1908. The label is molded into the glass. *Figure 21. C-1*

quently commissioned by other *parfumeurs*, department stores, and couturiers—to be added.

By 1912, less than a decade after establishing his Maison de Coty, one of Coty's *tarifs* (or price lists) mentions New York, London, and Moscow offices in addition to the Paris address. In that *tarif-général*, Lalique bottles for two scents are offered: *Cyclamen* and *Ambre Antique*, the latter one of the first Lalique designs for Coty. In all probability, the first Coty–Lalique collaboration was for *L'Effleurt de Coty,* or *Caress of Coty* (Figure 21), a bottle significant not only for its early date, which is 1908–10, but for its arresting decoration as well, one of the strongest of all Lalique's designs. Its rectangular body is molded on the front with a frosted and brown-stained panel that is dominated by a sinuous female nude who emerges full-blown and long-limbed from among the attenuated petals of a flower blossom and billows up into the ethereal sky. Like Venus arising from her shell or Daphne metamorphosing into a tree, this erotic flower creature is very much at one with magical, even mystical nature. The words "L'Effleurt de Coty" are molded along the bottom of this image. The tall stopper of an organic design is covered with a stylized Egyptian scarab, and almost seems incongruous with the motif on the bottle. Another reference to the classical world, though more to quotidian Athenian life than Greek mythology, decorates the tapering cylindrical body of the aforementioned *Ambre Antique* (Figure 22), dating from 1910. Lovely female figures in long robes with swept-up hair bearing floral bouquets are molded in bas-relief and stained with a red-brown *patine* (applied after the glass is taken out of the oven, unlike most enamel coloring, which goes on before the piece is fired and is fused by the heat), as is the stylized flower blossom stopper.

Arguably the most important design for Coty is the lovely *L'Entraînement* (Figure 23),

A pair of early René Lalique designs (circa 1910), one for Coty and the other Maison Lalique. Left: *Ambre Antique* for Coty with brown-stained Grecian maidens. Right: *Cigales* for Maison Lalique with long-tailed cicadas in molded design. Maison Lalique bottles refer to René Lalique designs sold without contents, to be filled by madame for her dressing table. Maison Lalique bottles were sold only through Lalique's retail outlets. *Figure 22. C-3, ML-475*

Very rare model. *L'Entraînement* for Coty. Male and female walking together on face, kissing on the reverse. Used for various perfumes. 1913. *Figure 23. C-2*

23

A famous Coty bottle, one of the first by Lalique, and a promotional Coty presentation for Galeries Lafayette. Far left: *La Feuillaison* for Galeries Lafayette in a standard square flask with button stopper. 1920s. Left: Flacon *Styx* for Coty with the four wasps on the stopper. 1910–13. *Figure 24. GL-1, C-4*

also known as *Le Baiser*. This flattened pear-shaped bottle with floriate button stopper has long been known from photographs and was illustrated as far back as 1912 in an article by Gustave Kahn in *Art et Décoration*. It is molded on both sides with two different scenes of the same couple clad in diaphanous classical robes. In his article "Lalique Verrier," Kahn singled out this oval flacon as one that, with its antique bas-relief and beribboned and floral borders, "the great designers of the eighteenth century would have loved" *("l'aiment les beaux artistes du XVIIIᵉ siècle")*.[11] He further continued his tale of the message on the bottle:

Un jeune Grec et son amoureuse s'en vont vers l'hy- ménée, vers l'amour, d'un pas envolé, sveltes, sou- riants, grands, saisis dans le rhythme de leur passion, deux branches enrubanées jettent au-dessus de leur têtes comme un arc de triomphe très léger, très subtil, qui semble non seulement les encadrer de sa joliesse,

mais les accompagner. Ils semblent s'élancer d'un arc de triomphe, d'une série d'arceaux fleuris agrestes, épais et ombreux vers des horizons de soleil et de bonheur.

Or loosely translated:

A young Greek and his love are walking on air going to their wedding and toward love. They are full of grace and mirth, caught up in the rhythm of their passion. Two limbs trimmed with ribbons extend over their heads like a triumphal arch, very light, very subtle, and it seems not only to frame them with its beauty, but to become a part of them. They seem to be flinging themselves up to the triumphal arch, through a series of flowered hoops, thick and shady, up toward the edges of the sun and the brink of happiness.

On the other side of the bottle, which has a colored *patine*, a kiss seals the love of the radiant young couple. This very rare bottle—one is in the Musée des Arts Décoratifs, Paris, another in the private collection of Marie-Claude Lalique—

One of the most coveted of the early Coty bottles is *Au Coeur des Calices* with the very realistic "bee" stopper. Blue glass of varying shades. 1912. *Figure 25. C-5*

was used for various Coty perfumes.

The bottle design *Styx* (Figure 24), also known as *Guêpes,* or *Wasps,* from 1910–13, is a slightly bulbous and fluted cylinder whose golden-stained stopper, molded with a quartet of wasps, wings spread and touching, sometimes comes with its stem separate, sometimes all in a piece. The bottle is very similar to Maison Lalique's *Carnette Fleur* (Figure 53), although that flacon's stopper is different, molded with flowers.

A bottle of an unusual shape and hue held the Coty scent *Au Coeur des Calices* (Figure 25), circa 1912. Of a delicate blue glass shading darker at the top and darkest on the stopper, which is in the shape of one solitary plump bumblebee, the bottle is of a rounded conical, or domed shape, with a regular, three-tiered pattern of ovoid dewdroplike petals molded on the outside and terminating on the neck with a dense mass of flower heads. Just as its name relates to that part of a blossom (the calyx) that yields the precious oils making up a scent, so Lalique's bottle has botanical and entomological verity as well as a poignancy and delicacy not usually found in his glasswork but more in his earlier goldwork.

Two bottles of Coty, *Série Epius* (Figure 26), also called *2 Lézards,* or *Salamandres,* from 1912, and *Masques* (Figure 27), 1913, are noteworthy for their stoppers, although the former's tapering lobed form is interesting for its two vertical rows of five graduated, thorny bumps on each of its sides. Its alternate name, *2 Lézards,* or *Salamandres,* derives from the rather horrific fan-shaped stopper molded with a pair of the confronting reptiles, which also decorates the flacon in Figure 101, *Mystère* for D'Orsay. The same bottle (and stopper) was used for the Paris, Chypre, and Styx scents and was available in three sizes. A sextet of handsome classical masks is molded on the rim of *Masques,* whose bottle is a squat version of the aforementioned *Styx;* the

25

M aison Lalique bottles on either side from *garniture de toilette* sets *Fleurettes* (left) and *Perles* (right). Each available in three scent bottle sizes. Second from left: *Série Epius* for Coty with design of lizards on stopper. Used for various perfumes. 1921. Third from left: *Feuilles* for Arys with stylized design on base and pointed stopper. 1922. *Figure 26. ML-577, C-6, A-1, ML-601*

elongated central knob of the stopper is topped with flowers.

The elegant bottle for Cyclamen (Figures 28–30) is an elongated hexagonal form tapering toward the neck on which a flat circular stopper, usually molded with the words "Cyclamen, Coty, Paris," sits. A round-ended triangular paper label in green and gilt, with the scent's name and "Coty" in fancy letters, is sometimes affixed to the lower body of the bottle. The decoration on the bottle itself is lovely: each facet features a tiny hovering nude holding a flower and with long, minutely membraned wings extending to the bottom of the flacon, over twice the length of their bodies. The hybrid woman-

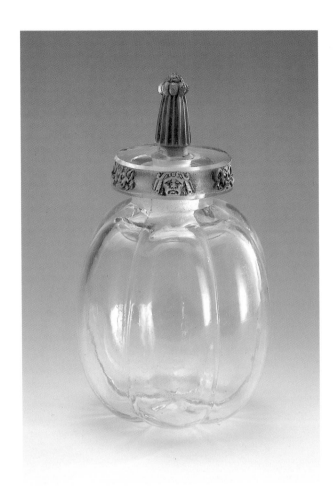

Rare René Lalique design *Masques* for Coty. Stopper comes with stem separate or as one piece. Possibly a very early Maison Lalique presentation as well. 1913. *Figure 27. C-7*

bottle, the remaining Lalique designs for Coty are undecorated, of rectangular, oblong, or, in the case of *Lipas Pourpre* (Figure 32), tapering square shapes. They are differentiated by and distinguished for their stoppers and labels, the former usually floriated and nicely complementing the bottle shape as with *Muguet* (Figure 29). By far the bottle most often produced for Coty is the aforementioned oblong-sectioned *Série Toilette* (Figure 18), which bore various signatures; it was available in three sizes and contained any of a dozen Coty scents. Its button stopper in frosted glass protrudes from a rather wide rim topping its neck and, again, organic designs are molded on it. This early bottle is one of the types referred to earlier as having been made at both the Legras glassworks and Lalique's own Combs-la-Ville factory. The Combs-la-Ville bottles, like others by Lalique, can bear a molded

insect creatures are clearly related to Lalique's jewelry, but here they are not at all threatening, like the *Dragonfly* corsage ornament in the Gulbenkian Collection, whose jaws emit the torso of a carved-chrysoprase woman. The fluttering fairies of *Cyclamen* are lovely, benevolent beings, more akin to Tinker Bell than Medusa. They are sometimes found with a light green or gray *patine*.

A tall frosted-glass eau-de-toilette flacon dating from the 1910s is for the Coty scent *L'Origan* (Figure 31); it is molded with an irregular floral garland that drapes itself around the soda-bottle-shaped body. Except for this decorated

The classic *Cyclamen* for Coty, sometimes referred to as "Libellule." The earliest version with "Cyclamen, Coty, Paris" molded on stopper. Later editions without "R." in signature. 1913. *Figure 28. C-8*

Two contrasting examples for Coty, the standard *Muguet* (left) and the beautiful *Cyclamen* (right). This *Cyclamen* model is with the plain stopper. 1920s. The *Muguet* has the squared shoulders, not to be confused with other similar but non-Lalique flasks made for Coty. 1910s. *Figure 29.* C-13, C-9

Combs-la-Ville were rented, and, according to Nicholas M. Dawes, he had a staff of between fifty and a hundred, involved "chiefly in the manufacture of commercial perfume bottles," whose "technology . . . was partly borrowed from the French wine and pharmaceutical bottle industries, including the molding techniques developed by Claude Boucher at his wine bottle and flacon manufactory in Cognac."[12] Boucher's innovative work methods, Dawes continues, included the revolving mold and *moule de bague* (ring mold) as well as new ways of getting glass into molds. The use of precision-cast metal molds was a major technological advance—

signature of the extended-*L* type; that is, the bottom part of the capital *L* stretches beneath the other six uppercase characters, pointing slightly upward at the end as if to neatly enclose the word. The Legras bottles, on the other hand, are unsigned and, with their higher lead content, clearer and crisper than the "softer" Lalique bottles, which trap more tiny air bubbles within. Incidentally, such bubbles were often thought to be imperfections in glass (certainly in crystal), but in Lalique and Coty's case, they were quite acceptable necessary by-products of a more inexpensive method of glass production.

Before proceeding with a discussion of Lalique's own bottles, retailed by Lalique's and other shops, a brief explanation of the techniques used by Lalique in making his flacons will be given. When Lalique first began manufacturing glass, in early 1909, his production facilities at

A third version of *Cyclamen* for Coty with a different neck/stopper configuration in contrast to Figures 28 and 29. Sometimes signed "Lalique Dépose," as in this example. *Figure 30.* C-10

borundum powder, whose application to glass results in a frosted, gritty surface and allows for the stopper to fit snugly into the neck of the bottle, yet be removed easily when desired (the inside neck is also coated with the powder). The technique of applying this substance is called *bouchon à l'émeri* and it was widely used by Lalique. Lalique also engraved a control number onto a bottle and its stopper, so two different numbers on two parts of a bottle is a sure indication they were not always together.

Glass is created by the fusion of a silica (such as sand, which Lalique employed, or quartz or flint) with an alkaline such as flux, soda, or potash (Lalique used the latter) in a kiln, or furnace. Metallic oxides can be added to give color to glass, and other elements will give glass hardness or luster. Lead oxide, for instance, lends it clarity, and the more of it that is added to the glass mixture, the more crystal clear the final product becomes. When the sticky mixture is in a molten state, it is then either blown into bubbles, which are given form by tongs or pincers, or it is made

more costly than wood or other materials, but allowing for the reproduction of a larger number of crisply cast products from a single mold. Dawes writes further, in his invaluable book, *Lalique Glass,* of two semiautomated methods Lalique used for his flacons: *pressé soufflé,* in which the glass is blown by mouth or bellows into a hinged two-part mold, and *aspiré soufflé,* in which the glass is sucked into a mold automatically by making a vacuum inside it. The earliest bottles were clear, flattened, and molded with a bas-relief motif (if at all), which was often tinted with a *patine*. Stoppers were of glass, although the occasional metal stopper appears on bottles originally designed by Lalique but often made later by another company. More often than not they were blown into a double mold and then fitted into bottles with the help of car-

Large eau-de-toilette bottles for Coty and Alpy. Left: *L'Origan* for Coty with frosted rings of rose blossoms. 1910s. Right: *Lavande* for the perfumer Alpy in a large flask with spreading branches. 1920s. *Figure 31. C-11, Al-1*

A Coty bottle used for *Lipas Pourpre* and other scents with waves design on stopper. 1914. *Figure 32. C-14*

to fit a mold. The final, and important, step is to anneal, or cool down, the mixture in a warm chamber or oven; this will prevent brittleness and give strength to the resultant solid substance. Lalique himself employed other nonautomated methods of making glass for his one-of-a-kind *cire perdue* pieces and massive architectural panels, which are explained in other books, among them Dawes's *Lalique Glass*.

The Maison Lalique bottles René Lalique designed, manufactured, and marketed solely under his own name, selling them void of contents so that the owner might decant whatever scent desired into them (or just use them on a dressing table or shelf as a decorative object), number seventy-eight different examples. Maison Lalique is a designation used by the authors solely to distinguish the pre-1945 house bottles

A simple but pleasing design for Coty's *Héliotrope*. Available with two stoppers as seen in the collection of Marie-Claude Lalique. *Figure 33. C-15*

Emeraude for Coty with flower decoration on frosted stopper and a clear oval flask base. This example came in a music box, which included a small replica of the plaque shown in Figure 19. 1910s. *Figure 34. C-16*

476 PAVOT 70 mm. 499 ANSES ET° 503 CARRÉ HIRONDELLES 498 3 GUÊPES 522 (LOTUS) HÉLÈNE
BOUCHON MARGUERITE 120 mm. 90 mm. 120 mm. 67 mm

Above: Five Maison Lalique offerings from the 1932 cat-alog probably designed in the 1920s. None of these examples has been available since 1945. *Figure 35.*

———— ◆ ————

Below: A grouping of Maison Lalique designs from the 1932 catalog. A photograph of *Marquita* in rich green color is also shown in Figure 41. *Figure 36.*

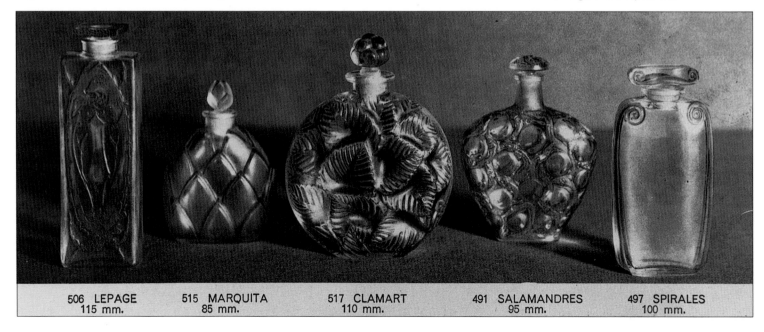

506 LEPAGE 515 MARQUITA 517 CLAMART 491 SALAMANDRES 497 SPIRALES
115 mm. 85 mm. 110 mm. 95 mm. 100 mm.

485 LENTILLE 50 mm.   518 PALERME 118 mm.   475 CIGALES 130 mm.   521 GRÉGOIRE 98 mm.   516 CAMILLE 60 mm.

Above: A 1932 catalog illustration of a quintet of offerings for Maison Lalique. *Cigales*, in the center, was designed in 1910 and is also shown in Figure 22. *Figure 37*.

———— ◆ ————

Below: Early designs from the 1932 catalog for sale in Lalique shops. Color illustrations of four of these models can be seen in Figures 40 and 62. *Figure 38*.

483 OLIVES 110 mm.   514 AMPHYTRITE 95 mm.   524 TANTOT 150 mm.   502 SERPENT 90 mm.   478 PETITES FEUILLES 102 mm.

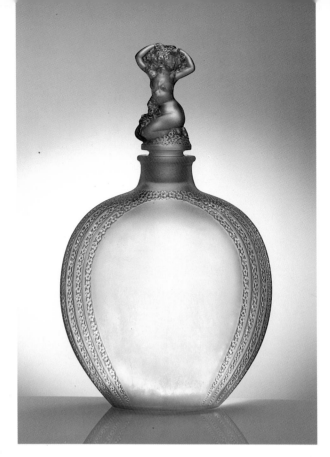

from the postwar Cristal Lalique models. In addition, there are nine designs created by Marc and Marie-Claude Lalique that are treated elsewhere and carry the Cristal Lalique house name.

For Maison Lalique perfume bottles, the most important resource for the collector is the 1932 publication produced by Lalique himself, the *Catalogue des Verreries de René Lalique,* which includes fifty-five of the Maison Lalique creations.[13] Invaluable for anyone interested in Lalique, the catalog pictures hundreds of pieces of Lalique glass—vases, tableware, boxes, figurines, automobile mascots, desk accessories, jewelry, and, of course, perfume bottles—and also gives their names and dimensions. Like all such ambitious publications, it has its errors here and there—especially in measurements—but it is still the best illustrated reference work of glass made by Lalique et Cie up to 1932. Unfortu-

Above left: *Myosotis* for Maison Lalique is one of the more elegant of the Art Nouveau designs. Three sizes were offered, each with a slightly different stopper. *Figure 39. ML-611*

Above: Two highly sought-after Maison Lalique scent bottles. Left: *Amphy-trite* (1922) with nude stopper. Also adapted as a commercial bottle for D'Orsay, Figure 106. Right: *Serpent* features a classical snake design. *Figure 40. ML-514, ML-502*

nately, the dates when pieces were introduced into the Lalique line are not listed, but it is safe to say that a good many of the pieces offered were being produced for at least ten years, if not two decades. Not all of the Maison Lalique bottles were illustrated in the catalog, for one reason or another (they were limited editions, they were not successful, or they were designed later, etc.), but the vast majority were shown. Some of those twenty-three flacons not depicted in the catalog will be considered in the following paragraphs and all are illustrated.

Most of the flacons in the 1932 catalog display figurative or floral motifs. They are of various shapes—ovoid, rectangular, spherical, etc.—and their sizes range from 2 inches (5 cm)—the height of the very squat, circular *Lentille* (Figure 37), whose diameter is considerably more than its height—to 11½ inches (29 cm) for

such as the scallop-shaped *Telline* (Figure 42), whose little stopper echoes the molluskan form of its body (see Figure 213 for another shell design, for a box holding a flacon).

One group of bottles is distinguished for its stopper type, an overflowing, horseshoe-shaped design that gently conforms to its usually tapering cylindrical body. In the catalog, these are all named after their tiara stoppers (*bouchons* in French), and they are *Bouchon Cassis* (Figures 43–45), *Bouchon Fleurs de Pommier* (Figure 46), *Bouchon Mûres* (Figure 54), *Bouchon Eucalyptus* (Figure 47), and *Bouchon 3 Hirondelles* (Figure 48). But for the latter, which depicts a trio of open-winged swallows, the cascading-stopper bottles depict flowers or leaves and branches. Appropriately, but rarely, the limbs of *Bouchon Cassis*, plump with currants, are of ruby-red glass (more often in blue), and, similarly, the mulberries of the *Bouchon Mûres* stopper have been molded in colored glass (a golden amber as well as an apt blue version is known). More often than not, these glorious stoppers have a delicate *patine* tint-

33

the tall eau-de-toilette bottle in the *Myosotis* (or *Forget-Me-Not*) pattern (Figure 39). Some bottles relate directly to other glassworks by Lalique—the snail-shell body of the nude-stoppered *Amphytrite* (Figure 40), the vase *Escargot* (see 1932 catalog, plate 7, number 931), the artichokelike *Marquita* flacon (Figure 41), and the similarly leafed *Armorique* vase (see 1932 catalog, plate 21, number 1000)—whereas others stand out on their own, without antecedents or imitations,

Above: *Marquita* for Maison Lalique in a beautiful rich jade green. *Figure 41.* ML-515

Right: *Telline* was a popular Maison Lalique design and was available in color. Illustration from 1932 catalog. *Figure 42.*

508   TELLINE   100 mm

Left, below left, and right: *Bouchon Cassis* is shown in red, blue, and black. The graceful tiara design was for Maison Lalique. Although all colors are rare, blue is more often seen. 1912–13. *Figures 43, 44, and 45.* ML-494

Right: *Bouchon Fleurs de Pommier* for Maison Lalique is one of the rarest and most sought-after of the tiara styles. *Figure 46.* ML-493

512 PLAT 6 DANSEUSES   507 BOUCHON EUCALYPTUS   511 PLAT 3 GROUPES 2 DANSEUSES

ing them. These bottles, incidentally, relate as a group to some *luminaires,* or table lamps, that Lalique designed, the *tiara veilleuse* type. These lamps too are dominated by their crescent tops, which are usually intaglio-molded with floral motifs, such as carnations, apple blossoms, roses, dandelion puffs, and almond blossoms as well as the figurative *(Cupids)* and avian ones (*Pigeons,* the lovebirds of *Inséparables,* seen also on Lalique frames).[14]

Figurative motifs on perfume bottles are less common than floral patterns, but several outstanding examples appear in the catalog. The aforementioned *Amphytrite* has a stopper molded as a crouching female nude (Amphytrite was the wife of Poseidon, god of the deep), and she tops a round flattened bottle molded with the cochleate outline of a whorled shell. Similar females in the guise of stoppers surmount the large ovoid bottles in the *Myosotis garniture de toilette* (Figure 39). The different-size bottles are topped by floral-bedecked women in vaguely suggestive poses, and the forget-me-not blossoms continue on down the sides of the bottles. Two similarly shaped compressed circular flacons, *Plat 6 Danseuses* and *Plat 3 Groupes 2 Danseuses* (Figures 47 and 49), depict nude dancers amid intertwining

*T*hree of the rarest and most beautiful of the Maison Lalique examples from the 1932 catalog. The authors have never seen *Plat, 6 Danseuses* on the left. See Figure 49 for color view of *Plat, 3 Groupes 2 Danseuses. Figure 47.*

*T*hree examples are known to exist of this spectacular Maison Lalique tiara scent bottle from the 1932 catalog. *Figure 48.*

floral garlands, and *Lepage* (Figure 36), a tall oblong bottle, is decorated with two attenuated nudes molded within a lozenge-shaped frame. The *Duncan garniture de toilette* includes four different-size bottles (Figure 50), square to oblong in shape, that feature central panels (within four gradated rectangular frames) of dancing female nudes, inspired by the dancer Isadora Duncan, in flowery settings. The narrowest flacon has a solitary figure; the next wider, a pair; the next, a trio; and the largest, which is nearly a square, a "chorus line" of four. Marc Lalique changed the mushroom-cap-like stopper shown in the 1932 catalog to a bold rectangular one in 1974 and it is still available in the current Cristal Lalique collection.

Méplat 2 Figurines (Figure 51), circa 1921, is a square-sectioned flacon with, again, two flower-surrounded female nudes in an oval center panel. The vaguely bow-shaped stopper is this bottle's outstanding feature, however: it is molded in delicate openwork and comprises two reclining female nudes who seem to float amid

496   BOUCHON 3 HIRONDELLES   120 mm

*P*lat, *3 Groupes 2 Danseuses* is a delicate design of extreme rarity for Maison Lalique. Figures molded on the inside. *Figure 49.* ML-511

*L*eft: A *garniture de toilette* set for Maison Lalique included four eau-de-toilette bottles in the *Duncan* design. The bottles were all the same height but came in four widths. The one-nude size, illustrated, was followed by the two-nude width and so forth. See Figure 244 for the revised-stopper version introduced in 1974 by Marc Lalique. *Figure 50.* ML-623

*R*ight: A rare Maison Lalique flacon from the 1932 Lalique catalog and one of the most valuable. Probably introduced in the 1920s. *Figure 51.*

garlands made of flowers and their flowing tresses. Such a stopper would be prone to chipping and breakage, and it is therefore no surprise that so few lacy types were made. *Bouchon Fleurs de Pommier* features openwork as well, and, interestingly, it and *Méplat 2 Figurines* were the two most expensive Lalique flacons in the 1932 catalog: *Pommier* was 500 francs, *Méplat* 450 francs, and most of the others were under 100 francs.

Pan (Figure 52) features classical masks more prominently than does the *Masques* bottle for Coty (Figure 27), whose neck is molded with faces. Here the satyr heads protrude from between floral garland borders and they comprise the main decoration on the tapering cylindrical body. Masks appear yet again on a later Guerlain bottle, *Bouquet de Faunes* (Figure 178).

Fougères (Figure 55) is a rectangular bottle with an oval "medallion" center molded on both

490   MÉPLAT 2 FIGURINES   120 mm.

492 NÉNUPHAR 120 mm.   520 AMÉLIE 73 mm.   504 PAN 127 mm.   523 AMBROISE 75 mm.   513 GLYCINES 120 mm.

Above: A group of five examples from the 1932 catalog for Maison Lalique distribution only. *Nénuphar* is seldom seen today. *Figure 52.*

———————◆———————

Below: A collection of Maison Lalique flacons. Two, *Bouchon Papillon* and *4 Soleils*, are illustrated in color in Figures 82 and 67, respectively. *Figure 53.*

77 A côtes bouchon papillon 60 mm.   486 Fleurs concaves 120 mm.   505 4 Soleils 75 mm.   510 Carnette fleur 120 mm.   482 Lunaria 80 mm.

494 BOUCHON CASSIS 110 mm.   501 GROS FRUITS 130 mm.   495 BOUCHON MURES 110 mm.

Above left and right: *Bouchon Cassis* and *Bouchon Mûres*, both very rare, as shown in the 1932 catalog. They are illustrated in color in Figures 43–45 and 74, respectively. In the center is *Gros Fruits,* also made for Volnay (see Figure 170). *Figure 54.*

Below: Three flacons for Maison Lalique. The highly popular *Cactus* design, still produced today, flanked by *Fougères* on the left, one of the most rare examples, usually in green but known in blue, and by the original version of *Rosace Figurines* on the right. *Figure 55.*

489 FOUGÈRES 90 mm.   519 CACTUS 98 mm.   488 ROSACE FIGURINES 110 mm.

Rosace Figurines for Maison Lalique with gold enamel set a record price, in excess of $20,000, for Lalique scent bottles at auction in 1988. Probably 1920s. Two known. *Figure 56.* ML-488

others, which also feature playful, floral-bedecked cherubs.

Rosace Figurines (Figure 56) is an ambitious figural bottle whose name makes one think of bigger things (*rosace* is *rose window* in French, although another meaning is simply *rosette*). Circular in shape with flat sides and a rectangular base, its form harks back to a Chinese porcelain model of the eighteenth century and, even further back, to a bronze prototype of the sixth century B.C.[15] Molded on the face of the flacon is an unlikely tableau comprising four sitting long-gowned neoclassical women whose arms conjoin and whose hands meet in the middle in a swastika configuration (this primitive religious symbol was associated with prosperity and good will). The bottle's stopper is in the shape of the wings of a moth. This flacon was made in clear and frosted glass, as so many of Lalique's flacons were, but at least two examples had a mustardy gold patination applied to them, according to Lalique expert and Paris art dealer Félix Marcilhac. One of these was sold at auction at the Hôtel

sides with the profile bust of a young woman, demure for a change and wearing a prim cap, all within a surround of fern fronds so symmetrically arranged as to appear semiabstract. This type of decoration appears as well on a Houbigant flacon for their scent *La Belle Saison* (Figure 166), but instead that bottle features leaves arranged radially and the profile is enclosed within a rectangle.

Enfants is a flacon presented with a matching *vaporisateur* (atomizer) and powder box in the current Cristal Lalique line much as it was in the supplemental section of the 1932 catalog (Figure 246). Looking more like a circular jar, it is molded all around with a continuous frieze of chubby putti, their uplifted hands supporting a canopy of three concentric gradational swags of rose blossoms, which end just at the plain neck and mushroom-cap stopper. Its lighthearted subject is reminiscent of turn-of-the century Wiener Werkstätte ceramics by Michael Powolny and

The 1932 Lalique catalog illustration of two distinctive models for Maison Lalique. *Figure 57.*

487 PANIER DE ROSES
100 mm.

484 CAPRICORNE
80 mm.

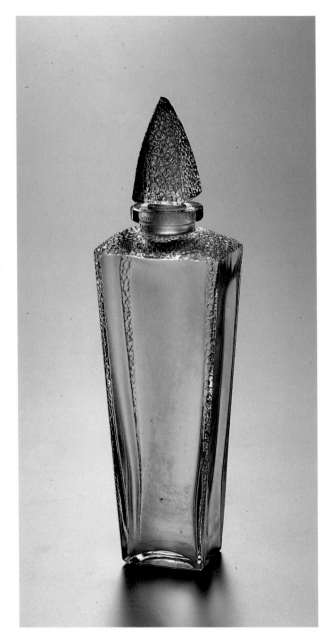

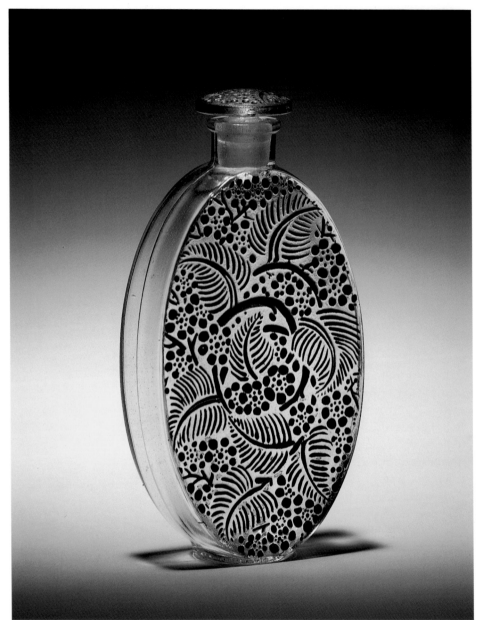

Unusual tapering flask, probably for Maison Lalique. Minute flower heads on sides and on pointed stopper. *Figure 58. ML-22*

Oval flask with black- enameled leaves in Art Deco motif. Probably for Maison Lalique. 1920s. Two known. *Figure 59. ML-13*

Bold heart-shaped flask with lizards. "Oreilles Lezards" for Maison Lalique. Two known. 1912.
Figure 60. ML-12

One of the most unusual and artistic of Lalique's
designs. Only three of this Maison Lalique design
are known to have survived, no doubt because of its
impractical proportions. Signature on both the base
and stopper. Probably 1920s. *Figure 61. ML-9*

The Birth of Lalique Perfume Bottles

A pair of Maison Lalique flacons of contrasting styles. Left: *Tantôt*, a late 1920s Art Deco design. Right: *Petites Feuilles*, introduced in 1914, with a more traditional motif.
Figure 62. ML-524, ML-478

42

swallows with down-sweeping, open wings, and the unusual, unnamed double flacon (Figure 207), its two rectangular bottles both topped with bird-design stoppers. *Salamandres* (Figure 36) features a swarm of the scuttling reptiles amid plump fruits.

Insects feature on the flacons *Capricorne* (Figure 57), *3 Guêpes* (Figure 35), and *Cigales,* or *Cicadas* (Figure 22). The trio of wasps on *3 Guêpes* does not, however, decorate the body of the squared cylindrical bottle: one wasp acts as a stopper, the other two are molded at the sides of the shoulders and are like little handles or ears. In this configuration they resemble the more specifically named *Anses et Bouchon Marguerite* (Figure 35), with three bouquets of daisy blossoms playing stopper and ears. *Capricorne,* despite its name, is a pear-shaped flacon decorated with several dark-gray-stained scarab beetles, their oversized antennae curling into giant vortices. The same design decorates the mushroom-cap

Drouot, Paris, in January 1988 for the staggering sum of 112,648 francs (just over $20,000). This established a record price for a production Lalique perfume bottle and is no doubt a sign of upwardly bound prices to come.

Animals show up less frequently on Maison Lalique flacons than do humans, although they appear on several stoppers topping nonfigurative bottles. Among those bottles largely featuring beasts is the earlier mentioned *Serpent* (Figure 40), its twisting, stained body filling the ovoid bottom, its open-jawed head forming its stopper. Besides the *Bouchon 3 Hirondelles,* avian designs adorn *Carré Hirondelles* (Figure 35), both sides of its square body aflutter with a flock of

Épines was one of the most popular prewar designs for Maison Lalique. Three scent bottles were part of a *garniture de toilette*.
Figure 63. ML-590

to the Art Nouveau style (as does Figure 59, with its black-enameled leaves). So too does *Nénuphar* (Figure 52), its squared body adorned with lily pads, a popular subject with the École de Nancy designers such as Émile Gallé and Louis Majorelle; they are all erect, upward-pointing leaves arranged in a strict pattern, however, making the flacon akin to what we think of as stylized Art Deco designs. Two lovely bottles, *Muguet* (Figure 64) and *Clairefontaine* (Figure 65), are reminiscent of Lalique's floral haircombs, which themselves were quite Japoniste, as so many Art Nouveau *objets* were. Their bodies are plain and undecorated, but their stoppers are delicate, naturalistic sprays of lily-of-the-valley. In fact, the bottles can be considered to be acting as vases to these tiny bouquets.

stopper. *Cigales,* dating to around 1910, is an elegant Japoniste creation whose oblong body is not at all geometric, but instead metamorphosed into an object of nature by four closed-winged cicadas, their membranes heightened with *patine,* which cling to the sides. The daisy button stopper is harmonious with the entomological subject below, and the feel of the bottle is rather Art Nouveau but for the configuration of the insect quartet, which is a cleverly constructed conceit and not at all realistic (see Figure 89, *Cigalia,* which also has a design of four cicadas).

Leaves and flowers in both ordered arrangements and asymmetrical disarray decorate the bulk of the bottles in the 1932 catalog. The random designs—such as the swarm of twisting lotus blossoms of *Tantôt* (Figure 62), the interlocking thorny branches of *Épines* (Figure 63), and the seed-filled *monnaie du pape* (or money plant) pods of *Lunaria* (Figure 53)—relate more

A pair of *Muguet* flacons from the Maison Lalique collection with very rare jade and lavender colors. *Figure 64. ML-525*

Clairefontaine, for Maison Lalique/Cristal Lalique with a free-form lily-of-the-valley stopper decoration, has been produced from the 1920s to the current day, signed without "R." postwar. *Figure 65. ML-526, CL-104*

500   COLLERETTE AVEC GLANDS SOIE   130 mm.

44

A rare Maison Lalique flacon from the 1932 Lalique catalog. Probably introduced in the 1920s. Silk tassels. *Figure 66.*

Stylized leafy forms are molded on *Olives* (Figure 38), *Petites Feuilles* (Figure 62), *Lentille* (Figure 37), *Clamart* (Figure 36), *Glycines* (meaning *Wisteria,* Figure 52), *Amélie* (Figure 52), and *Ambroise* (Figure 96), flowers on *Lotus (Hèléne)* (Figure 35), *Panier de Roses* (Figure 57, molded as a lovely basket of the blossoms), *Dahlia* (a *garniture de toilette* with four flacons, Figure 247, the front of the round flasks formed as one flower head), *Fleurs Concaves* (Figure 53), and another *garniture de toilette, Fleurettes* (Figure 26). Some bottles appear to have precedents in nature, but their designs are so regular and stylized as to rank as abstract. These include *Camille* (Figure 37), whose spherical body is molded with half-emerging concertinaed fan forms. There is no doubt that the dark-enamel-tipped protrusions covering the spherical bottle and matching stopper of *Cactus* (Figure 55) are meant to be the ends of the prickly plant, but their regular arrangement has turned them into a decorative pattern not necessarily one with nature. *Cactus* was also offered as a limited issue by Rotterdam Lloyd, marked "Royal Dutch Mail."

Palerme (Figure 37) and the *garniture de toilette* called *Perles* (Figure 26) are flacons with purely decorative design, neither natural nor abstract. Swags of graduated beads are draped along the tapering cylindrical forms (*Palerme* available in polished glass, *Perles* in clear or satin glass). This simple but elegant motif is one that was popular with other Art Deco designers and related to the contemporary taste in interior decorating, which itself harked back to the ornamental garlands of eighteenth-century France. Along this same line, two other bottles should be mentioned: *Gros Fruits* (Figure 54) and *Collerette avec Glands Soie* (Figure 66), both of which are marked by the long silk tassels meant to overflow onto the surface on which they sat. Such glossy threads or ropes (which were attached to their side ears) were exotic Oriental touches much favored by Art Deco designers, from couturiers like Paul Poiret to furniture designers like Émile-Jacques Ruhlmann and Paul Follot.

The stunning *4 Soleils* (Figure 67), circa 1913, depicts four molded chrysanthemum medallions, each made radiant by colored foil,

4 *Soleils* for Maison Lalique is one of the most admired and unusual flacon designs. The four insets are backed with foil to reflect light in a dramatic fashion. *Figure 67. ML-505*

Lovely statue of a draped girl on a sphere for Maison Lalique. Clear base except for molten raised and frosted free-form portion below neck. D'Orsay version (Figure 105) has frosted/striped base. *Figure 68. ML-18*

Shapely oval flasks with stained blossoms. Probably Maison Lalique. See drawing *Lalique par Lalique*, EDIPOP, Lausanne 1977, page 156. *Figure 69. ML-21*

whereas those from the 1932 catalog retain their original catalog numbers (400s–600s). Postwar models are identified as Cristal Lalique in this system and are number coded beginning with 100 (CL-101, CL-102, etc.).

There also exist numerous Lalique drawings depicting flacons (see Figures 71 and 72), some never realized, others created as is, or, rarely, with slight alterations. It is easy to see from these drawings just how precise and talented a draftsman Lalique was. His incredibly exact renderings rate highly with discerning collectors today for their beauty as well as for their rarity. Often of pen and ink or pencil, they could be highlighted with gouache, wash, or watercolor. A lovely unfolding lotus blossom design, never realized by all accounts (see Figure 71), reveals an

which backs them and is trapped within the glass. Lalique also used foil on some of his glass jewelry pieces and at least one known vase. The simple button stopper is molded with four thorny twigs and the bottle itself has a squat conical shape with a rounded-off bottom. It was available in a lovely and unusual frosted-pink hue.

Bottles that did not appear in the 1932 catalog include the very rare flacons that may have been deliberate limited editions, those that were created after 1932, as well as those that were made in large numbers in the 1910s and '20s but for some reason or other were taken out of production. In the Appendix, these Maison Lalique bottles have been numbered (ML-1, ML-2, etc.),

Imposing bottle with hexagonal base and free-form frosted stopper. Black enamel on edges of base. Probably for Maison Lalique. *Figure 70. ML-23*

unusual stopper in the shape of an elephant. See too the discussion of flacon drawings illustrated in Sigrid Barten's book on Lalique's goldwork, page 25.[16] Plaster models were sometimes also used to produce experimental molds, most likely for the prototypes that were made before mass production commenced (or for one-offs). Plaster models exist today of Lalique flacons (see Figure 73), which helps to corroborate this hypothesis.

Among the rarest and most significant Maison Lalique bottles are *Satyr*, with its devil-head stopper and horns extending out as stems (Figure 74); the oval *Satyr/Masque*, distinguished by its

Four designs by René Lalique for scent bottles that, to our knowledge, were never produced. These examples are elaborate and, had they been introduced, would have been among the most admired. They were probably created in the 1910s. *Figures 71 and 72.*

46

donutlike stopper (Figure 75); *L'Églantine de la Reine,* with a tiara stopper molded with dog roses (Figure 76), as well as two unnamed magnificent crescent-type flacons (Figures 77 and 78). *Deux Marguerites* (Figure 79), comprises a double-flower-head shape and was likewise produced after the war by Cristal Lalique.

Another Maison Lalique flacon of special interest is known as *Jeunesse,* or *Cherub* (Figure 80), and is unique in that its stopper has a figurative stem, or dauber, molded as a nude putto, which extends into the cylindrical bottle. Such types of stems were not all that unusual in *parfumerie*—a

A collection of artifacts that illustrate Lalique's process of design from drawing to model to finished product. The swirling flacon in the center was never introduced. The label on the left was used extensively by D'Orsay on the Lalique bottle. The maquette for an atomizer base was made commercially. *Figure 73.*

Czechoslovakian-made (circa 1930) bottle for Ramsès eau de toilette has such a nude female dauber—but within René Lalique's *oeuvre* it is very rare.

A fascinating experimental flacon in the collection of Marie-Claude Lalique (Figure 81) is in a protracted-arch shape and is molded on the inside with the shape of a showy carnation. When the liquid is poured into the flacon (the illustration shows the bottle filled with turquoise-colored water), it fills in the floral outline, revealing the blossom (in this case in a brilliant hue).

Two of the more dramatic examples for Maison Lalique in the 1910s and '20s. Left: *Bouchon Mûres*, mulberry tiara stopper in amber/orange. Right: *Satyr*, devillike face stopper with horns protruding. Both very rare. *Figure 74. ML-495, ML-5*

A mask of satyr with horns on an oval flask with donut stopper probably for Maison Lalique. 1910s. Only one known. *Figure 75. ML-20*

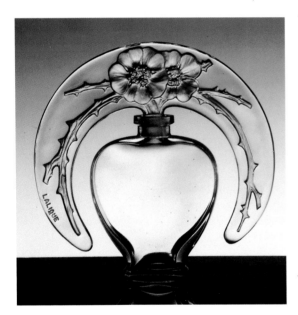

The flower-blossom tiara flacon *L'Églantine de la Reine* was for Maison Lalique. Extremely rare. *Figure 76. ML-8*

The delicate small-blossom tiara was probably for Maison Lalique in the 1910s, but discontinued prior to 1932. Only one known. *Figure 77. ML-14*

This tiara design with large blossoms is the only one known of this Maison Lalique flacon. Probably 1910s. *Figure 78. ML-15*

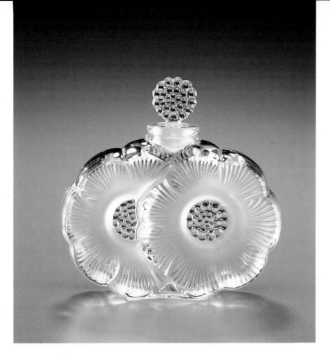

Deux Fleurs, or Deux Marguerites, designed 1935–36 for Maison Lalique, signed "R. Lalique." Available from Cristal Lalique postwar without "R." Figure 79. ML-1, CL-108

Three examples of Lalique's versatility. Left: Jeunesse with the nude cherub for Maison Lalique. Rare. Center: Lilas for Gabilla with a multitude of tiny flowers. 1926. Right: Narkiss, or Althéa, designed for Roger et Gallet in the 1910s. Flower in center with enamel. Figure 80. ML-0, Gab-3, R&G-1

Demilune base with startling blue carnation motif. Experimental. Figure 81. EX-1

Two late Art Nouveau designs from the early 1920s. Left: An elegant purse-size perfume flacon, 2 Sirènes, for Maison Lalique. The only purse-size made pre-1945. Right: Bouchon Papillon for Maison Lalique with butterfly design on stopper. Figure 82. ML-4, ML-477

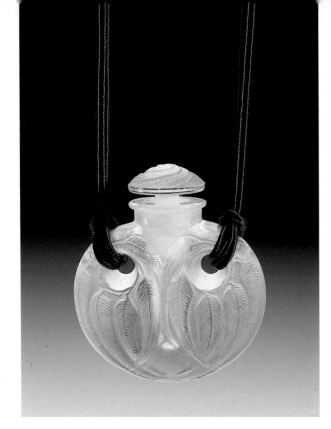

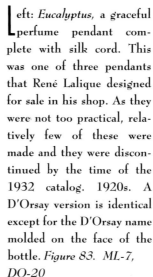

Left: *Eucalyptus*, a graceful perfume pendant complete with silk cord. This was one of three pendants that René Lalique designed for sale in his shop. As they were not too practical, relatively few of these were made and they were discontinued by the time of the 1932 catalog. 1920s. A D'Orsay version is identical except for the D'Orsay name molded on the face of the bottle. *Figure 83.* ML-7, DO-20

Right: Elegant pendants of bullet shape, decorated with flowers, probably Maison Lalique. 1910s. Extremely rare. *Figure 84.* ML-19

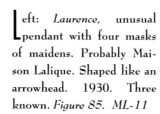

Left: *Laurence*, unusual pendant with four masks of maidens. Probably Maison Lalique. Shaped like an arrowhead. 1930. Three known. *Figure 85.* ML-11

Right: *Sirène*, a magnificent molded design of a mermaid, probably Maison Lalique. Also see Figure 87, which shows the correct stopper. Circa 1920. *Figure 86.* ML-16

Left: An illustration of *Si-rène* for Maison Lalique with the correct stopper from "L'Art Décoratif Française"—Editions Albert Lévy, 1918–25 Revue. Figure 86 shows the only known base to this bottle. *Figure 87. ML-16*

Below: Lovely pair of oval flasks with sunburst design. Left: Very rare Maison Lalique model with stylized disk stopper. Right: Experimental version with plain stopper. *Figure 88. ML-17, EX-5*

An interesting quartet of tiny perfume containers is included in this Maison Lalique group, three designed as pendants and one as a purse-size flacon. These miniatures were an interesting sideline of Lalique's glass production and are quite rare today. They were probably not especially popular when they were first marketed, which accounts for their scarcity. A pair of nude nymphs amid branches is molded on *2 Sirènes* (the purse flacon, Figure 82), tree branches form *Eucalyptus* (Figure 83), flowers decorate a colorful arrowhead-shaped cylindrical example (Figure 84), and possibly the loveliest of all is another arrowhead-form pendant with a long-haired woman's head on each of its four sides (Figure 85). A later pendant, for the *parfumeur* Raphael (Figure 148), has an acorn-shaped bottom with a gilt-metal screw-top cap.

51

CHAPTER 4

Lalique's Growth in the Perfume Industry

THE MAISON LALIQUE CREATIONS AND THOSE bottles made for Coty over a period of several decades together comprise an impressive *oeuvre,* one that any glass manufacturer would be proud of. But for Lalique it was not enough—and his services were much in demand by the 1910s, especially after his proven success with Coty, the premier *parfumeur* in Paris. Indeed, the decade following World War I, a period of *joie de vivre,* was to witness a massive upswing for the fragrance industry in France, largely as a result of the ever-widening American market. As Nicholas M. Dawes has written:

> The industry earned a new respect and status. Attracted by commercial potential and artistic respectability, numerous fashion houses and couturiers began to manufacture and market perfumes. By the 1920s *parfumerie* was considered an admirable and respectable branch of the decorative arts.[1]

Lalique's role in the upsurge was not ignored by his contemporaries, with Gabriel Mourey noting that:

> . . . between 1908 and 1918 he designed bottles in hundreds of shapes, all most ingenious,

Cigalia, the commercial version of the famous *Cigales* (Figure 22) for Roger et Gallet. Unique pressed-wood box for the next smaller size also illustrated. 1911.
Figure 89. R&G-6

charming, and modern, turning them out from the factory literally to the tune of several millions. He thus brought about a real revolution not only in the glass industry but in the perfume trade also. . . . Here was Lalique's dream in process of realization.[2]

The 1925 Exposition des Arts Décoratifs et Industriels Modernes in Paris was another milestone for the perfume industry and for Lalique, both of which were heavily represented at the fair. Not only did Lalique display a wide variety of flacons in his own pavilion, but his talents were in evidence as well in the Section Française of the Parfumerie pavilion, where a great number of his commercial designs were shown and where he was employed as an interior designer for Roger et Gallet, the perfume company, and for whom he created display cases and furniture in addition to flacons. In a September 1925 article, Maximilien Gauthier called the Roger et Gallet display a "refuge of tranquillity and discreet luxury, where there rules the mystery of a sweet brightness which is amenable to the infinite expansion of the scents."[3] A spray of glass blossoms hung over the stand and the floor was of exotic wood with glass insets. The furniture, ac-

53

A magnificent *cire perdue* vase by Lalique, circa 1912. Polished except for the sweeping cicadas that are still in the *cire perdue* texture with black enamel and bulging clear eyes. The cicadas motif was used extensively by Lalique in his various presentations, including perfumes (Figures 22 and 89). Molded as one piece. *Figure 90.*

cording to Gauthier, was "simple and somber," allowing all the light to shine on the four vitrines, where one viewed "the impeccable perfume bottles aglow."

The Exposition was indeed a runaway success for the by-now sexagenarian Lalique. He also designed an exterior fountain for the fair and a dining room in the Sèvres pavilion, further securing his place as the premier *maître verrier* in Paris and as one of its distinguished designers.

It is no surprise that the *Rapport Général* on the 1925 Exposition, published in September of the same year, chauvinistically boasted of France's preeminence in the fragrance industry:

The taste for perfume has spread throughout every social class. Decorative bottles and boxes

are no longer found exclusively in de luxe shops; they can be seen in innumerable storefronts in Paris and the provinces and appear in the most modest households. Designs by French artists are everywhere, at home and abroad, where the perfume industry is but a vehicle to aid the spread of French taste.[4]

Likewise, a 1919 article by Henri Clouzot sings the praises of Lalique and French *parfumerie*:

. . . *Car le grand verrier a son usine, dont il surveille la marche avec un soin jaloux. On lui commande ses créations par dizaine de mille à la fois, et c'est rester au-dessous de la vérité que d'estimer à un million le nombre de flacons revêtus de sa firme depuis dix ans. . . . Ne l'oublions pas, d'ailleurs, la parfumerie de luxe française tient une place de premier rang sur les marchés étrangers. Pour ne parler que des États-Unis, nos exportations . . . sont arrivées a plus de 500 millions en 1914, et nous pouvons espérer . . . une augmentation bien plus importante, la concurrence austro-allemande supprimée.*[5]

A loose translation goes:

. . . The great glass master has his own factory, whose progress he oversees with jealous care. He orders the creation of tens of thousands of perfume bottles at a time, and it's an understatement to estimate that a million perfume bottles have been produced by his firm in the past ten years.

. . . Moreover let us not forget that *de luxe* French perfumes have a place of the first rank in foreign markets. To mention just the United States, our exports . . . have added up to more than 500 million [francs] in 1914, and we can hope for an even larger increase once our Austro-German competition is eliminated.

The numbers—of both flacons and francs— are indeed huge for well over half a century ago, but compare them to today's statistics and they constitute small change. According to a recent article, the fragrance industry in France, which presently employs some 33,000 people, had a turnover of 28 *billion* francs in 1986, a third of this amount from the export trade, where perfumes rank fifth (behind agrochemistry, armaments, tourism, and automobiles).[6]

In the period just before World War I, Lalique began to produce flacons for several other *parfumeurs* besides Coty, including Roger et Gallet, D'Orsay, Arys, and Rosine, all of whose Lalique flacons will be discussed in this chapter, followed by the other pre–World War II commissions, from *parfumeurs,* couturiers, and department stores, in France and abroad.

Roger et Gallet was mentioned earlier in connection with Jean-Marie Farina (né Johann Maria Farina in Cologne), whose firm the cousins Armand Roger and Charles Gallet acquired in 1862 from a relative named Colas, who himself bought the firm in 1840 from the family of the original founder. Roger et Gallet received its first official award in 1867 and was given similar recognition at many subsequent international expositions. By the turn of the century, Roger et Gallet was without rival in the production of violet-scented perfumes, but a decade or so later its concerns were expanding to concentrate not only on what went in their bottles, but what was on them, as well as how they looked.

A history of the firm (located today in Bernay, northwest of Paris in Normandy, and part of Sanofi, the French healthcare corporation) has been put together by its archivist, J. F. Davy, and sheds light on the Lalique–Roger et Gallet collaboration, which lasted from 1910 to 1922 (although Lalique bottles were still being produced later).[7] The year 1910 is cited as being a year "especially rich with new product . . . which marked a new stage in the evolution of [the firm's] products." Four top-of-the-range perfumes are said to have "forged an alliance

One of Lalique's best designs for Roger et Gallet, *Paquerettes,* with a graceful tiara of daisies. 1910s. *Figure 91. R&G-2*

with the plastic arts, the decoration and graphics . . . of the time," these being Psyka, Cigalia, Narkiss, and Paquerettes (Daisies). Although the exact circumstances of how Lalique and the *parfumeur* connected are not known, proximity no doubt again played a part: Roger et Gallet's showroom was located at 8 Rue de la Paix, very close to René Lalique's shop at 24 Place Vendôme.

Of the four bottles, all of which are quite rare, *Cigalia* (Figure 89), introduced to the market in 1911 and depicting a quartet of Japoniste cicadas clinging to its rectangular sides, is the most interesting. It is similar in concept and motif to Maison Lalique's *Cigales* flacon (Figure 22), although that model's longer and narrower

56

Two designs for Roger et Gallet seen in *La Renaissance de l'Art Français et des Industries de Luxe*, 1919, page 30. Left: *Salvia* only known from this illustration and the 1920's Roger et Gallet catalog. Right: *Psyka* also shown in Figure 93.
Figure 92. R&G-7, R&G-8

Psyka for Roger et Gallet with elegant butterfly label and decorated box.
Figure 93. R&G-8

Paquerettes's being of the tiara type molded with a baker's dozen of daisy blossoms and *Psyka*'s being of the pointed variety, but *Narkiss* (Figure 80) has a lovely bottle and stopper (it is sometimes known as *Althéa*, which may have been its Maison Lalique name). Its heart-shaped body is molded on both sides with a solitary flower head, which is highlighted with dark enamel between its petals, lending them a butterfly-wing-like look, which nicely corresponds to the two pairs of butterflies comprising the domed stopper. A charming leatherette box shaped like the flacon, embossed with a large flower head and "Roger et Gallet Narkiss," encases this lovely bottle.

One later Roger et Gallet scent bottle, *Flausa* (Figure 94), introduced around 1915, though in development as early as 1911, was an exclusive production, and not even a vaguely similar bottle exists. The flask form is molded with a lovely

body may be more elegant. However, the veined-leaf stopper of *Cigalia* complements the gray-stained membraned wings of the insects much more nicely than the floral button stopper does *Cigales*. What distinguishes *Cigalia*, however, is its presentation box of cardboard with a light brown pressed-wood veneer on which are impressed two green-tinted cicadas (in some cases, the box is painted green, the insects with a silver wash), whose bodies surround the nicely stylized relief letters "Cigalia/Roger et Gallet/ Paris." The bottle was available in three sizes and there was a matching cicada-molded face cream jar as well. See Figure 90 for a classic Lalique *cire perdue* vase utilizing the cicadas motif with great success, also from the 1910–12 era. This vase is a good example of how Lalique used a motif first in his jewelry and then repeated it in his perfumes as well as in other forms of his glasswork.

Paquerettes (Figure 91) and *Psyka* (Figure 92 and 93) are both distinguished for their stoppers,

a showy tropical bird flying amid a mass of intertwining branches, the latter of which also decorate the domed stopper. Its opalescent jade-green hue is an obvious reminder of its scent's name, "Le Jade," after the semiprecious stone that was the favored material for classic eighteenth-century Chinese snuff bottles, although glass proved the most popular medium. This makes Lalique's bottle a conceit of sorts—glass imitating stone, perfume imitating snuff (which, after all, was another type of scent). Lalique also designed the handsome cardboard container for this scent and a matching powder box as well. The square boxes are printed in dramatic black, green, and gold hues, and there are lovely Lalique labels, too, comprising a roundel with two stylized golden birds enclosing the name and maker. Another box's stop is embellished with a trio of the same tropical bird molded on the bottle. Such durable handmade containers of cardboard were inaugurated by François Coty before 1910 and other *parfumeurs* soon followed suit, eschewing the plain but expensive silk and leather boxes they had often used in the past (mass-produced, machine-made boxes started to be made in the 1920s). Now the container as well as the contents could advertise the scent and its maker—and both could be equally appealing to the olfactory and visual senses. In Roger et Gallet's case, the gilded bird-of-paradise motif went even further than a perfume bottle and box. Indeed, around 1926 the interior of their Paris showroom at 38 Rue d'Hauteville (in the 10ème arrondissement) was covered top to bottom with this same lush tropical scene, from carpet to walls to vaulted ceiling.

Another handsomely packaged Lalique creation for Roger et Gallet that dates from 1926 (introduced in the United States in 1929) was *Pavots d'Argent*, or *Silver Poppies* (Figure 97). Its oval flask body is molded with two overlapping flower heads, whose rich ruffled form is echoed

semidraped female figure, half kneeling, half sitting amid a bower of blossoms and foliage. Her left hand is innocently raised to her bared breast and she is bending to smell a fragrant flower. An ochre-colored stain highlights the flacon's face.

Le Jade (Figure 96) is one of Lalique's most striking, if derivative—*inspired* is perhaps a better word—flacons. Introduced in 1923 were both an eau de cologne and perfume of this Far East-derived scent, the former in a non-Lalique-designed rectangular bottle with a craquelure surface (reminiscent of Oriental porcelains), the latter in a stunning Lalique container, an unabashed reference to Chinese snuff bottles (and proof of excellent marketing sense as well on the designer's part). Its shape is that of a snuff bottle and its molded image is exotic and Far Eastern—

Two outstanding flasks in the Art Nouveau style. Right: *Flausa* for Roger et Gallet with molded design of a robed girl. "Flausa" molded on face and "Roger et Gallet" on reverse. Signature on stopper. 1910s. Left: *Rosace Figurines* for Cristal Lalique. Same four-nymphs design on base as Maison Lalique version (Figure 56). Two-nymph stopper by Marc Lalique, also used on Cristal Lalique stemware in the early 1950s.
Figure 94. CL-110, R&G-5

several times over in a slightly geometrized version on its matching cardboard carton, also signed "R. Lalique" and printed in stunning pink and silver with black highlights. This scent was touted as "The fragrance of your sweetest dream," and a 1927 advertisement featured an ethereal, semidraped woman lost in a cloud of silver blossoms.

At least twenty Lalique bottles were made for Parfums D'Orsay, founded around 1830 by Count Alfred D'Orsay, apparently an aristocratic man-about-Paris who was also blessed with "a great nose" for blending scents. The

Rose Rouge for Roger et Gallet, together with Lalique display sign for Roger et Gallet. Original seal, perfume, label, and box add dramatically to the rarity and value. *Figure 95. R&G-9*

early formulas were popular for generations, and by the 1910s D'Orsay's scents were being exported to the United States. Lalique was commissioned to design some of their flacons; others were made by Baccarat, Verreries Brosse, and Süe et Mare. D'Orsay too (sometimes known as La Compagnie Française des Parfums) was located near Lalique's Place Vendôme showroom —at 17 Rue de la Paix[8]—and indeed the exterior and interior of this large space was designed by La Compagnie des Arts Français, the top Parisian interior-decorating firm run by the aforementioned Louis Süe and André Mare.[9] Besides de-

signing an impressive façade dominated by stylized floral swags—a popular theme in Parisian Art Deco that had its roots in eighteenth-century French decoration but that was no doubt intended to evoke floral essences as well—the talented pair furnished the showroom with exquisite furniture sheathed with exotic wood veneers, with tasteful vitrines inset into arched niches, and even with perfume bottles—for instance, the handsome hexagonal design in black glass for the scent Dandy, introduced in 1926. Lalique designed a presentation set for this scent; see Figure 100, also in black glass.

Lalique's association with D'Orsay likely began in 1913, with a black glass bottle (also available in clear glass) for the scent *Ambre D'Orsay* (Figures 101–103). This architectonic

Above: A pair of rich green flacons from the 1920s. Left: *Le Jade* for Roger et Gallet, designed like a Chinese snuff bottle. Right: *Ambroise* for Maison Lalique, decorated with overlapping petals pointed upward. *Figure 96. R&G-3, ML-523*

Left: *Pavots d'Argent* was created by Lalique in 1926 for Roger et Gallet; it features a flower blossom spreading to the edges of the flask. *Figure 97. R&G-4*

Right: Classic presentation created for D'Orsay, *Poésie D'Orsay*. Blue stain with draped-maidens decoration. 1914. *Figure 98. DO-7*

squared cylindrical form with its caryatidlike corners is among Lalique's loveliest figurative designs and is especially elegant in black. It does seem that black flacons are especially favored by D'Orsay, judging from the abovenamed Süe et Mare and Lalique bottles as well as *Mystère* (Figures 101 and 104), another opaque black-glass Lalique creation,[10] this from 1915. This flacon has a quasi-cubed form with a narrow angled neck and wide flat top. The stopper has a protruding stem molded with four lizards (this bottle is also known as *Lézards,* and a clear version may have been offered by Maison Lalique), echoing the undulating reptilian frieze on the rim below it. An elegant red-and-black octagonal leatherette box with the name D'Orsay in gold superimposed around the "O" holds this *Mystère* flacon.

Other Lalique bottles for D'Orsay are much more lighthearted and more lightly colored than the black examples mentioned. Two are rare commercial versions of Maison Lalique bottles —one a frosted sphere molded with a pinnate pattern surmounted by a long-robed maiden, her

Roses D'Orsay, a cylinder with a metal band of Grecian figures. Glass cover with stopper inside. Crystal by Baccarat, metalwork by Lalique. Signed "RL" in metal. 1912. *Figure 99.* DO-13

Important presentation set for D'Orsay with flacon *Dandy.* Four perfume bottles and one powder box in fitted presentation case, all in black glass with crest of D'Orsay in center of box. Late 1920s. One known complete. *Figure 100.* DO-14

hands clasped to her breast (Figure 105); the other *Le Succès* (Figure 106), similar to the figural-stoppered, nautilus-shaped *Amphytrite* (Figure 40). *L'Elégance* (Figure 107) is a nearly square bottle molded with two rather suggestive maidens in diaphanous gowns dancing *en pointe* amid a full floral surround. The scent Ambre also was available in this bottle, which had a red-brown stain covering most of its background.

The small but spectacular tiara-stoppered flacon for the scent *Leurs Ames* (Figure 108) is molded on its exaggerated crescent (which almost fans down to its base) with two sensuous female nudes hanging from a blossoming tree. The lithe women sport upswept hairdos and are Art Nouveau in feel, as is the craggy-branched tree, which resembles forms seen in Lalique's Japoniste goldwork. At auction in Paris in January 1988, one of these bottles sold for 58,184 francs (over $10,000). This bottle has also been seen without "Leurs Ames" molded on its lower front, which leads one to believe it may have been sold by Maison Lalique. In 1940, it ap-

Three of the seven flacons that Lalique is known to have made in all-black glass. Left: *Le Parfum NN* for Forvil. 1920s. Three known, only one complete with box. Center and right: The classic *Ambre D'Orsay* and *Mystère* for D'Orsay, with Grecian figures and lizards designs, respectively. "Ambre D'Orsay" molded on lower edge of the former. 1913 and 1915, respectively. *Figure 101. F-1, DO-1, DO-2*

4 Figurines, unusual clear version of *Ambre D'Orsay* (Figure 101) but with eagle stopper. *4 Figurines* is the Maison Lalique version and probably preceded the commercial model for D'Orsay. Seen in fitted Maison Lalique box. 1913. Rare. *Figure 102. ML-3*

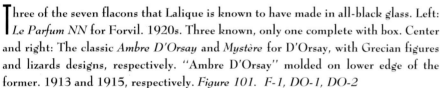

A comparison of the *Ambre D'Orsay* and *4 Figurines* designs. The standard black with the floral design on the stopper and the clear flacon with four eagles on the stopper. The latter signed intaglio, upside down. 1913. *Figure 103. DO-1, ML-3*

A comparison of the black and clear versions of *Mystère* for D'Orsay. The clear example is much more difficult to find, has a script signature, and may have been a Maison Lalique presentation rather than a commercial bottle. 1915. *Figure 104. DO-2*

Left: Lalique's stopper design of a maiden on a sphere is a classic for D'Orsay. Note that the base is lined and frosted in contrast to the Maison Lalique version in Figure 68. *Figure 105. DO-3*

Right: *Le Succès* for D'Orsay is a very rare commercial version of the Maison Lalique flacon *Amphytrite* shown in Figure 40. The configuration of the base is changed and the figure on the stopper is in a different pose. 1910s. *Figure 106. DO-6*

Left: *L'Elégance* aptly describes this flacon for D'Orsay. Dancing nudes on one side, plain on the other. 1910s. *Figure 107. DO-5*

Right: The elegant *Leurs Ames*, created for D'Orsay, with large tiara stopper. Sometimes found without "Leurs Ames" molded into bottle. 1913. *Figure 108. DO-9*

63

peared as a plastic novelty piece commemorating the twenty-fifth anniversary in the United States of D'Orsay; it contained the perfume Belle de Jour.

Floral designs appear on several D'Orsay flacons. The perfume *Grâce D'Orsay* (Figure 109) is contained in a triangular bottle; two isometric triangles cling to its sides like ears and give the bottle an overall square silhouette. These ears are in fact openwork floral designs with a brown *patine,* and similar blossoms adorn the triangular stopper, which tops a long neck. This very rare flacon was illustrated in a 1920 French fashion journal, *L'Illustration des Modes,* but it was probably introduced some five years earlier. *Le Lys* (Figure 110) was available in four sizes, its rounded bottle studded on the side with pert floral blossoms whose leaves and stamens can be highlighted with red, brown, or blue *patine.* The circular stopper, decorated with the same bloom

Elegant array of Lalique flacons for various perfume companies, dating from 1910s to 1950s. *Le Lys* for D'Orsay (center), a popular floral design with various stains in four sizes. Molded "Le Lys D'Orsay" on stopper. 1920s. *Figure 110. DO-11*

The globular *Chypre* for D'Orsay with stylized flower design and matching button stopper. 1920s. *Figure 111. DO-10*

A sample tester for the use of store personnel to offer their clients various D'Orsay fragrances. Molded "D'Orsay" and "R. Lalique." In addition, each of the stopper/daubers is molded with the number and name of each different perfume. *Figure 112.*

as on the bottle (not very lilylike, despite its name), is molded with the words "Le Lys D'Orsay" in a circle around the center. A similar mass of flower heads appears on a glass powder box for D'Orsay, which, under the *Émiliane* name, appears in the 1932 catalog (plate 49-bis, number 70); sometimes both the base and lid were molded with the blossoms, sometimes just the cover. *Chypre* (Figure 111) was available in two sizes, a design of large flower heads molded all over its globular body.

Another interesting item made for D'Orsay was a five-piece perfume tester, the only such multicompartment perfume receptacle known to have been designed by Lalique (other tester bottles were separate bottles packaged in a set). The rectángular tester base (Figure 112) has an *Épines* (Thorns)-style motif all over except on its stopper tops, which are molded with flower heads. "D'Orsay" is molded on the front of the base, and each stopper, which was named and numbered at its center, terminated in a little dauber,

A set of three *Série Roses* for D'Orsay in a black leather silk-lined box. The "standard" D'Orsay flask by Lalique. 1910s. *Figure 113. DO-8*

Left: *Illusion* for D'Orsay gives the appearance of a box. Under the cover, however, is a regular stopper. *Figure 114. DO-15*

Right: *Rose Ambrée* is a 1920s design for D'Orsay. Five recessed and beaded columns on each face. *Figure 115. DO-12*

L a l i q u e ' s   G r o w t h   i n   t h e   P e r f u m e   I n d u s t r y

Left: A commercial bottle for D'Orsay perfume of unknown name with a "double dot" border design on base. Same stopper as in D'Orsay Figures 115 and 117. *Figure 116. DO-16*

Right: Square flask with single dot borders for D'Orsay. Same base as Figure 113. Same stopper as in D'Orsay Figures 115 and 116. *Figure 117. DO-17*

Left: Oval flask for D'Orsay's *Gavotte Bleue* with blue botton stopper. Silk cord through hole in stopper ties around neck. *Figure 118. DO-18.*

Right: Tall, shapely flask with blue enameled borders of flowers. Eau de toilette for D'Orsay's *Chypre*. *Figure 119. DO-19*

which allowed madame to sample the scent in the shop where the tester was displayed. Such elegant testers replaced earlier models of wooden frames holding plain glass bottles.

Less decorated bottles were produced in large numbers for D'Orsay. These include the so-called *Série Roses* (Figure 113), the standard D'Orsay flacon of square shape with floral stopper available in two sizes (and with at least seven different scents); *Illusion* (Figure 114), a clear squared-off design with beaded edges and a floral design over the stopper cover (roses or cornflowers); and *Rose Ambrée* (Figure 115), which had five beaded columns on each side.

Another fairly early link was forged in the late teens between Lalique and Arys, which was

Three distinctly different models for Arys from the 1920s and '30s. Left: *L'Amour dans le Coeur* with a heart design and a cupid in the center. The larger size is without the center design. Center: *Faisons un Rêve* with beading on base and ball stopper. Right: *Croyez Moi* with molded circles of leaves on a sphere.
Figure 120. A-5, A-3, A-6

located at number 3 Rue de la Paix and was known for its Oriental-inspired fragrances. In a 1925 publication, the so-called "Société Anonyme des Parfums d'Arys," whose products were prepared "according to the formulas of Dr. Reymondon," is singled out as "one of the most powerful organizations in France and in the whole world."[11] Its modern factories (in Courbevoie as well as Milan, Barcelona, Brussels, Budapest, and elsewhere), the report goes on, are equipped with "laboratories developing equipment which is marked by its perfection, and constantly updated in accordance with the latest mechanical methods."

The bottles Lalique designed for Arys do not rank among his most beautiful—they are

without the verve, vitality, and the *je ne sais quoi* some of his bottles for Coty, D'Orsay, Roger et Gallet, and others possessed. *Feuilles* (Figure 26) is quite common, a tapering flask form molded all over with regular vertical rows of skeletal leaves; its pointed stopper, also leaf-covered, is its saving grace. Dating from 1922, it also held the scent Faisons un Rêve. The bulbous, spade-shaped *L'Amour dans le Coeur* (Figure 120), from 1919, was available in two sizes, the larger bereft of its distinguishing feature—that is, a stained, heart-shaped central medallion enclosing the silhouette of a winged Cupid, arrow at the ready. A frosted-glass sphere with matching stopper was designed for Arys's *Croyez Moi* (Figure 120)

Three of the fourteen flacons René Lalique designed for Arys from the mid-1910s to mid-1930s. Left: A tapering cylinder with pointed stopper and a stylized base design. Center: *Le Lilas* in a heart shape with floral stopper. Right: *Un Jour Viendra.* An oval flask with border design. The latter also in a larger version without border design (Figure 219). *Figure 121. A-8, A-4, A-9*

before 1922, with four horizontal strands of tiny rosebuds. Altogether, Lalique designed at least fourteen flacons for Arys, nine of these available in more than one size.

Parfums Rosine, mentioned earlier, was influential and eclectic couturier Paul Poiret's perfume branch, one of many nonfashion endeavors in which he indulged. At least one bottle for Rosine's scent *Nuit de Chine* was designed by Lalique (Figure 127), and a larger version of this long-necked flask with a slightly different flame stopper was marketed by Fragonard, which was also connected to Poiret. Since Poiret proudly promoted his creations as being totally conceived by him, it is unusual that he decided to have the

Left: Art Deco tapered cylinder with conical stopper for Arys. Beading decoration as with other Arys examples. Early 1920s. *Figure 122. A-10*

Right: A tapered cylinder with a button stopper for an unknown perfume by Arys. The beading decoration is also carried out in two other Arys models, shown in Figures 120 and 122. 1920s. *Figure 123. A-13*

Below: An unopened example of *Rien que du Bonheur* for Arys, a simple but pleasing design from the early 1920s. *Figure 124. A-12*

name Lalique associated with his flacons, which were generally manufactured in Italy under his close supervision. Even more interesting is the fact that a Roger et Gallet scent, *Persana,* appeared in the same bottle, this example being the same size as the Fragonard flacon. Poiret himself designed a Murano-made bottle for Nuit de Chine in a Chinese snuff bottle shape of the same type as Lalique's *Le Jade* for Roger et Gallet, only in clear glass with gold highlights and an amethyst-hued button stopper.

The House of Worth was another major Lalique client in the 1920s and later. Maison Worth was established by British-born Charles Frederick Worth (1825–95) in Paris in 1874. Recog-

This attractive cylindrical bottle decorated with butterflies is for Arys, probably from the 1930s. It was also available with butterflies on the stopper only. *Figure 125. A-7*

fashionable ladies in France, Britain, other parts of Europe, and America. After Charles Frederick's death, the House of Worth continued to flourish under the guidance of his sons, Gaston and Jean-Philippe. It was the latter who originated the idea of creating scents under the fashion house's name, and that idea came true in 1924 under the aegis of Charles Frederick's great-grandson, Roger Worth, who founded Les Parfums Worth.

In the 1920s and 30s, Lalique designed numerous bottles for Worth scents, with seemingly countless permutations and variations of flacons and stoppers for the scent Dans la Nuit (In the Night), which Jean-Philippe Worth had created. Worth was not the first fashion house to create perfumes—Poiret had done that a decade earlier, and Gabriella "Coco" Chanel had launched her famous No. 5 around 1921—but it was certainly

nized today as the father of *haute couture,* Worth settled in Paris in 1845, working first as a sales assistant for Madame Gagelin, renowned for her silks, satins, brocades, and other sumptuous fabrics. In 1858 Worth and his Swedish backer/partner Otto Bobergh opened their firm, Worth et Bobergh, at 7 Rue de la Paix, from which four generations of Worths would operate.[12] The Franco–Prussian War forced the closure of the establishment in 1870, but it was in limited business soon thereafter, now known simply as Maison Worth, Bobergh having gone back to Sweden. Worth's elaborate, heavily ornamented dresses were worn by the Austrian Empress Elizabeth, by France's own Empress Eugénie, by the Duchess of Marlborough (Consuelo Vanderbilt), by Russian royalty, by Eleonora Duse, Sarah Bernhardt, Nellie Melba, Adelina Patti, Mrs. J. Pierpont Morgan, and countless other

Rose, with coiled thorns stopper, for Arys. Stopper frosted and with stain, otherwise clear. *Figure 126. A-14*

Pair of almost identical designs for three different companies with frosted "flame" stopper. Larger bottle used for Fragonard and for Roger et Gallet's *Persana*. Smaller version with slightly different stopper: *Nuit de Chine* for Rosine. 1913. *Figure 127. Fr-1, Ros-1, R&G-10*

many guises in reality represent dozens of separate and distinct bottles. Figures 129, 130, and 15 show that the moon, stars, sky, and chevrons are the principal members of the tableau presented, although not always together. The loveliest bottles are those of dark blue enameled over frosted glass molded with a sprinkling of tiny stars all over their spherical bodies, with disc stoppers molded with a crescent moon, the scent's name, and some stars, or just the moon and stars without the letters (the name usually appeared on a round paper label attached to a string tied around the neck). This latter stopper type was available from the mid-1920s through the mid-1930s, according to Worth, but it was discontinued after that time due to a complaint lodged by the American firm Procter & Gamble, which alleged it was too much like its Ivory soap logo and therefore constituted trademark infringement. Worth altered the stopper, which was from then on molded without the stars.[14]

one of the originals, and other fashion houses followed fast in their footsteps. By the 1930s, it seemed that all the top couturiers' dressing rooms were equipped with the "house scent," beautifully packaged in art glass flacons by Brosse, Baccarat, Lalique, and others.

The scent Dans la Nuit, with its flowery, amber fragrance of black currant, iris, jasmine, rose, and tuberose over a musky bottom note,[13] was Worth's first excursion into the world of *parfumerie* and was introduced around 1924–25. Its flacon's basic design concept, courtesy René Lalique, is simple and elegant, appropriate and evocative. Since so many other scents were packaged in the same flacons as Dans la Nuit, including Je Reviens, Vers Toi, Vers le Jour, Sans Adieu, and Projets, virtually the entire repertoire of Worth's fragrance menu, the style of bottle is considered the generic Worth style, although its

A model in glass of the Lanvin logo. Molded "R.L." as was often used in 1920s Lalique production. The Lalique logo piece was probably used as a promotional item by Lanvin in the form of a *cachet* and a *cendriee*. The famous Lanvin black bottle with the stopper and the logo in gold were designed by Armand-Albert Rateau. No scent bottles are known to have been designed by Lalique for Lanvin. *Figure 128.*

71

Another variation is the rounded flat flacon with upright disc stopper, which was available in clear glass, in cobalt blue (the color of the actual glass, not the enamel, and this for Dans la Nuit only), in medium blue, in a rich amber shading to orange, with or without a chevron design on the body, with a chevron motif on the stopper (for Vers le Jour), and, very rarely, in clear green or turquoise. Of all Lalique's bottles, this *Dans la Nuit* type represents one of the largest groups—and one most available to collectors. The unusually colored flasks or the ones sporting stoppers from the other Lalique/Worth selections rank among the rarest.[15]

For the sophisticated scent Je Reviens, created in 1932 by Maurice Blanchet and containing "fresh green top notes, the essences of jasmine,

Four distinctive designs with strong Art Deco flavor. At extreme left and right: *Vers le Jour* variations for Worth. Both bottles with chevron design, the one with a metal stopper. Center left: *Parfum A* for Lucien Lelong. A chrome case with black or brown enamel on bottle and case. Sometimes called *Skyscraper*. Center right: *Tzigane* for Corday.
Figure 129. W-3, LL-1, Cor-1, W-5

hyacinth, tuberose, rose, and ylang-ylang, with mellow smokey undertones,"[16] Lalique designed one of his first modernist bottles, available in four sizes (Figure 131). A fluted blue glass cylinder, its neck steps up in three segments to meet an aqua button stopper. The later models had a cylindrical ribbed stopper, which Marc Lalique designed in 1952 because customers apparently had a difficult time removing the button version. The bottle is strongly architectonic in its appearance and far removed from the romantic figural flacons for Coty and Roger et Gallet of nearly two decades earlier. The use of another material, plastic, for the stopper in later years was also unusual for Lalique, although he is known to have designed a square celluloid box (Figure 132) molded with cherries (though he did not actually

A grouping of the cobalt-blue family of flasks for the Worth perfume *Dans la Nuit*. The large bottle has a stopper with a crescent moon and stars that was the style prior to the change in 1936 to avoid conflict with the logo for Procter & Gamble's Ivory soap. Signed with "R." postwar and reintroduced with "Creation Lalique" in 1985. The small flacon in front is a tester. *Figure 130.* W-2, W-103

Left: A grouping of bottles for the highly successful *Je Reviens* created for Worth, showing the button and ribbed stoppers. Ribbed stopper designed by Marc Lalique in 1952 to make the stopper easier to remove. Signed without "R." postwar. *Figure 131. W-101, W-6, W-101*

Below: An example of René Lalique's versatility and innovation was his mid-1920s work in plastic, as shown with this powder and rouge box. Had this material been economically available earlier in his life, he would have probably made greater strides in this direction. *Figure 132.*

elegant contemporary statement. *Imprudence* (Figure 134), too, available in three sizes (as was *Sans Adieu*), is marked by its semistepped disks sometimes tipped with silver. These make up the entire bottle and give it the appearance of a Japanese pagoda, which may have been intentional, since advertisements for this scent (launched quite late, in 1938) show it nestled in a Japoniste setting, amid blossoming cherry trees.[18] As with *Je Reviens,* in 1952 Marc Lalique redesigned the original 1930s stopper, in this case from circular to square, the latter being easier to open. Lalique also designed the handsome fluted cylindrical box for Imprudence, of midnight blue leatherette cardboard with gold trim. A handsome geometric bottle was designed for *Vers Toi* (Figure 135), whose tapering cylindrical body had a zig-zag or dentate pattern at its base, and whose two-tiered stopper sported a similar motif. It was also called *Pot de Fleurs,* but its rather rigid rectilinearity was devoid of any plant life. Also, a condiment bottle designed by Lalique is quite similar to this flacon.

manufacture it or the aqua stopper). Indeed, by the 1930s Lalique had largely veered away from his earlier busy patterns, had forsaken his Art Nouveau roots almost completely and turned to the present, or to the future, designing bottles that were often devoid of *femme fatales* and other frills. The chevron design on many of Worth's bottles, too, was very moderne-looking, a chic[17] Art Deco pattern, playing on the letter *W* for Worth.

Sans Adieu (Figure 133), introduced in 1929, was also a stark modernist flacon, a green glass cylinder with a smart stopper comprising five graduated disks ending in a button top. One writer has likened the stepped stopper to a stylized pine cone, and the wood-veneered box it often came in is a good argument for its possible organic reference, but, taken as a whole, it is an

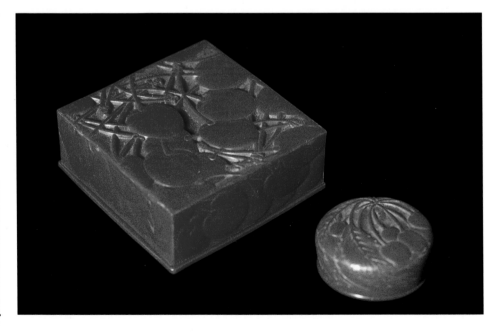

*S*ans Adieu for Worth in two different green presentations. Left: The set of three in regular *Sans Adieu* flacon with tiered stopper. Right: The all-purpose Worth flask in the seldom-seen green and with a *Sans Adieu* stopper. 1929 introduction. Also made postwar until the 1950s without "R." in signature. Many sizes. *Figure 133. W-8, W-106, W-2, W-104*

L a l i q u e ' s   G r o w t h   i n   t h e   P e r f u m e   I n d u s t r y

The flattened ovoid horizontal flask of *Projets* (Figure 136), known in the United States as *Clear Sailing,* is an unusual one among Lalique's flacon repertoire, with its molded sailboat (sporting a "W" insignia on one sail) set in a pattern of stylized waves. This nautical scene is rather lighthearted and gay, as is the concave floral motif molded all over *Lilas* (Figure 137), an ovoid flask with flowered disk stopper that also held the scents Rose, Öeillet (Carnation), Jasmin, and Gardenia. Available in four sizes, the bottle was introduced in the late 1930s, probably as late as 1939.

Several of the Worth bottles were produced after Lalique's death, into the 1950s, some with altered stoppers, as on *Je Reviens* and *Imprudence,* others more or less as they originally were. Also, the *Dans la Nuit* star-dusted globe and cobalt blue flask were reintroduced in 1985, signed

Left: Two clear bottles for Worth. Left to right: the *Dans la Nuit* sphere without enamel. 1920s. *Imprudence* with the tiered bottle and the pre-1952 stopper. 1938. Both models also made early postwar without "R." in signature. *Figure 134. W-1, W-103, W-7, W-107*

Right: *Vers Toi* for Worth, also known as *Pot de Fleurs.* 1933. Right: The richly butterscotch postwar example, *No. 7,* or *Tortues,* for Morabito, designed by Marc Lalique in 1951. *Figure 135. W-11, Mor-1*

"Creation Lalique." The blue scallop-edge *Requête* flacon (Figure 226) has been attributed to René Lalique, but experts at Worth have confirmed it as a Marc Lalique design. Lalique's commissions from Worth were not all flacons. Soon after his success at the 1925 Paris Exposition, he designed the House of Worth's showroom at Cannes. Lalique provided a great deal of both architectural and interior design work for the black marble building, from the leaf-decorated frosted-glass door frame and front sign (both of which were illuminated at night) to an innovative type of cornice lighting, which was to replace hanging fittings. It consisted of glass panels of quarter-round sections with decorative molding on the convex outside.

Parfums Forvil, a large French *parfumerie* whose showroom was located on the Rue Castiglione and whose factory was in Nanterre,

Above: A 1936 United States introduction, *Projets*, for Worth. *Figure 136. W-10*

Left: *Lilas* for Worth, a very popular model with an attractive design of indented daisies. Late 1930s. *Figure 137. W-9*

Right: A brilliant green version of the standard Worth flask for the perfume *Sans Adieu* in the 1930s. Also made postwar until the 1950s without "R." in signature. *Figure 138. W-2*

Lalique's Growth in the Perfume Industry

commissioned some thirteen flacons from Lalique, many of which held more than one scent. One of the most significant—and rarest—of the Forvil bottles was for *Le Parfum NN* (Figure 101) and *Le Parfum Noir* (Figure 141), the same but for the molded letters of their names. Like some of the opaque glass bottles for D'Orsay, this rectangular flacon is all black except for a white wash covering the name and the frieze of concentric arcs running along the top, where the lid comes off to reveal the stopper. This pure rectangle—which in itself looks like a box—was available in a chic red leather case, making it an *objet d'art* more like a precious jewel than a scent bottle. Most likely it was available in a limited edition and was very costly. The simple modernist design of this bottle was in stark contrast to another rare Forvil flacon, this more in the organic Art Nouveau mode: *Le Corail Rouge* (Figure 144), whose name was molded on its rectangular front and enameled in red, like the skeletal bits of coral covering it. Bits of knotted, knobby twine highlighted in black enamel wend their orderly way around the five glass cabochons of *Les 5 Fleurs* (Figure 145), from as early as 1926. This was also known as *Celtic* because of its interlaced design, common to medieval Celtic art. The box is a stunning red, black, and gold Art Deco rectangle.

The elongated-cube flacon *Trois Valses* was

Above: Egg shape with stylized "W" design for Worth. Extremely rare. *Figure 139. W-12*

78

JE REVIENS

LES PARFUMS

WORTH

PARIS

Left: A striking advertisement by Parfums Worth for *Je Reviens*. Based on the use of the button stopper, the advertisement appeared prior to 1952. *Je Reviens* was introduced in 1932. *Figure 140.*

Right: A very rare black glass example, *Le Parfum Noir*, for Forvil. Molded lettering with white stain. Same as Figure 101, *Le Parfum NN*, except for name of perfume. Stopper is under top cover. 1920s. *Figure 141. F-2*

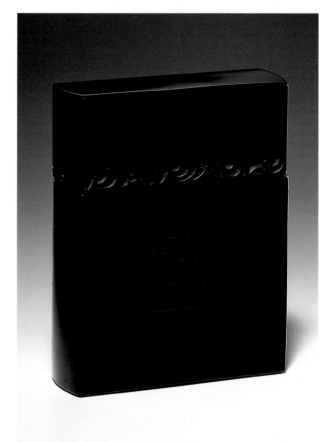

molded with a square central panel of a pair of putti (it was also known as *Frise d'Enfants*), the relief touched with gold. This and *Anémones*, sometimes known as *Narcisse* with its four large concave flower heads, are shown in Figure 146. Another flacon, *Les 5 Fleurs* (Figure 147), also known as *Daisies*, is similar to D'Orsay's *Le Lys* (Figure 110) and Maison Lalique's *Émiliane* powder box. *Chypre*, or *Wisteria* (Figure 148), is a slender cylinder molded with flowering wisteria vines and a mushroom-shaped stopper to match.

An interesting round flask bottle (Figure 149), is molded all over with beaded spirals. Sometimes known as *Coquilles*, it was available in four sizes and held Relief or Les 5 Fleurs eau de Cologne. Also with a bead design is the bottle known as the *1925 Flacon* (Figure 150), a cylinder molded with black enamel beadlike strands and reminiscent of the columns flanking the Porte de Concorde entrance of the 1925 Paris exposition.

D'Heraud was a Parisian *parfumeur* about whose history little is known, although Lalique did provide at least twelve bottles for the firm,

Above: The jeweler influence is apparent in *La Perle Noire* for Forvil. Simulated glass pearl in center with matching stopper and in center of original box. 1922. *Figure 142. F-4*

Above right: *Les Anémones* for Forvil with enamel in flower centers. Design like vase number 1179, 1932 Lalique catalog, and current Cristal Lalique vase number 11613—*Deux Anémones*. 1925. *Figure 143. F-11*

Right: *Le Corail Rouge*, a startling and extremely rare red-enamel coral design for Forvil. 1920s. *Figure 144. F-3*

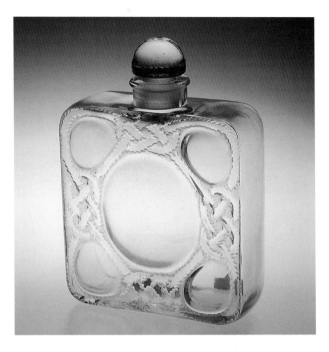

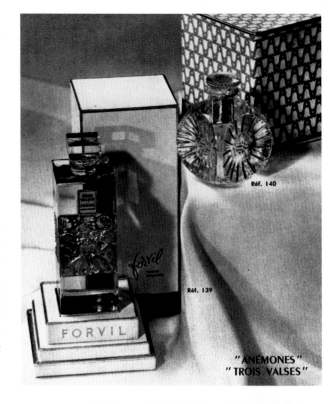

Right: Two unusual and rare designs for Forvil as illustrated in an early 1930s Forvil catalog. Left to right: *Trois Valses*, with a molded frieze of children, and *Anémones* (or *Narcisse*), with four deeply indented flower heads. *Figure 146. F-9, F-10*

"ANÉMONES" "TROIS VALSES"

all in the 1920s. Many *parfumeurs*, as was mentioned earlier, produced one or several scents in a few seasons but were not able to succeed against the vast number of competitors and therefore were bought up by another firm or shut down and were never heard from again. The bottle for the scent *Phalène* (Figures 152 and 153) harks back to Lalique's early Art Nouveau creations, although it was introduced in the United States in 1923 and probably a year or two prior to that in France. It is in the shape of a butterfly with outstretched wings, but its body is that of a woman, making it akin to Lalique's hybrid human-insect jewels. It was available in a lovely orange-amber shade of glass (this flacon was sometimes called *Amberina*) as well as frosted with black stain. It has either a floral-blossom stopper or a disk-shaped one (this latter only on the amber version). Interestingly, a similar bottle was designed by Lucien Gaillard around 1914, but the shape of the flacon was triangular, the hybrid creature's wings pointing

Right: Leather, satin-lined box of three perfumes for Forvil, containing Les 5 Fleurs and other scents. Frosted and stained pattern of daisies on cylinder base and disk stopper. 1920s. *Figure 147. F-5*

Left: Two postwar presentations and one pre-1945. Left: *Réplique* for Raphael with acorn shape. Right: *Coeur Joie* vial of hearts for Nina Ricci. Both created by Marc Lalique. *Coeur Joie* had a four-, three-, two-, and one-heart size. In the center, *Chypre* for Forvil, which has wisteria draping down the bottle. 1920s. *Figure 148. R-101, F-7, NR-106*

Right: *Relief* for Forvil was a very popular model from the 1920s. *Figure 149. F-8*

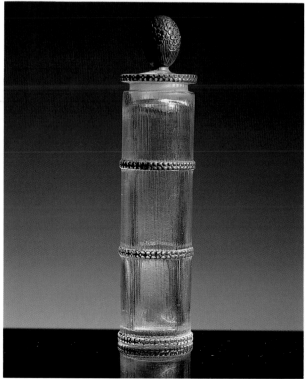

Left: A replica of columns at the entrance of the 1925 Paris Exposition serve as an extremely rare flacon for Forvil. Black-enamel decoration on the four beaded bands and teardrop stopper. *Figure 150. F-12*

Right: A simple but distinctive and rare design for "5" by Forvil. *Figure 151. F-13*

Lalique's Growth in the Perfume Industry

Left: *Phalène*, an Art Nou-veau design of a nude with dramatic butterfly wings for D'Heraud. Concave floral stopper. 1923. *Figure 152.* DH-2

Right: Two colorful flacons for Worth and D'Heraud. Left: *Vers le Jour* in the stan-dard Worth flask with or-ange glass and chevron stopper. 1930s. Right: *Pha-lène* for D'Heraud with the darker-colored center, shad-ing to orange edges. The stopper differentiates it from the other *Phalène* de-sign in Figure 152. Often called *Amberina* in orange. 1923. *Figure 153. W-2, DH-3*

Left: A rectangular flask for D'Heraud with Greek-key motif. Molded "Lotion" on face and "O——" (probably "Origan") on reverse. Also molded "D'Heraud" and "Paris" on sides. 1920s. *Figure 154. DH-8*

Right: *Chypre* was created for D'Heraud and the in-dented columns are usually stained brown. The perfume and company name are molded on the stopper. 1920s. *Figure 155. DH-5*

Left: *Origan D'Heraud* for D'Heraud from the 1920s. The names are molded into the faces of the flask. *Figure 156. DH-7*

Right: *Violette D'Heraud* was probably designed in the 1920s. Perfume and company name molded on face, one on each side. *Figure 157. DH-6*

Left: *Semis des Fleurs* for D'Heraud. Indented flower heads with floral stopper similar to *Phalène* (Figure 152), also for D'Heraud. 1923. Extremely rare. *Figure 158. DH-9*

Right: *Marjolaine* for D'Heraud from the 1920s with the face of a lady in the mold. *Figure 159. DH-11*

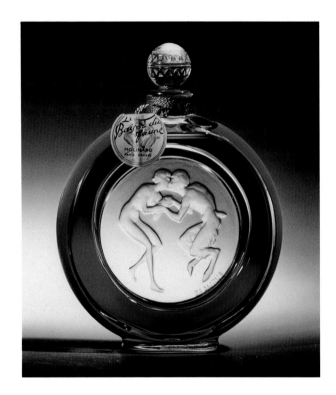

The prizewinning *Le Baiser du Faune* created by René Lalique for Molinard in 1930. Made until the early 1950s with the "R. Lalique" signature. *Figure 160. M-1*

A popular flacon for Molinard of graceful nude dancers. Generally called *Calendal* but known by several names and used for various perfumes. 1929. Made until early 1950s and signed "Lalique" after 1945. *Figure 161. M-2, M-101*

1894 with the head office in Paris, first near the Stock Exchange in 1920, then in 1930 at 21 Rue Royale, on the corner of the Faubourg Saint-Honoré. In the 1920s and 30s, the firm expanded considerably, in large part due to its collaboration with Lalique and also because of its introduction of solid perfumes, or concreta, whose bases were natural floral waxes.

Le Baiser du Faune (Figure 160), also known as *Embrasse* and *Légende,* was created in 1928, the floral scent itself launched in 1930. The name was inspired by Mallarmé's poem, *L'Après-midi d'un faune,* which was later set to music by Claude Debussy and then interpreted in dance by the great Russian ballet star Nijinsky. The flattened circular bottle features a central medallion of a faun kissing a forest nymph, both molded in frosted glass, and this large roundel is surrounded by a donut-shaped form. This is the part of the flacon holding the perfume. The globe stopper is molded with straight lines and

downward (this was for Clamy's scent Femmes Ailées). Gaillard was a contemporary of Lalique's who was a jeweler/glass designer.

Two other flacons of particular interest were made for D'Heraud: *Semis des Fleurs* (Figure 158), its spherical body molded with concave flower heads, and *Marjolaine* (Figure 159), its rectangular body molded with a woman's left-facing profile head in a center square, highlighted with a brown *patine.*

Although only five flacons were designed by Lalique for the *parfumeur* Molinard in the late 1920s and 30s, each is a unique design not repeated elsewhere in Lalique's massive repertory. All are molded with neoclassical figures of the type found on Lalique's vases. Since 1849, Molinard was headquartered in Grasse, where it still flourishes today. It began as a small shop offering "scented waters" in Grasse's main square, setting up a factory to distill and create perfumes in

Madrigal was designed in 1930 for Molinard and was in production until early 1950s. Signed "R. Lalique" pre-1945 and "Lalique" postwar. *Figure 162. M-3, M-102*

chantes (see 1932 catalog, plate 20, number 997), although those women are more frenzied and erotic than the plump dancing nudes of *Calendal.* This flacon is noted too for the fact that it was embellished with several colored *patines,* including pastel pink, blue, and green. This beautiful bottle was presented in two different boxes—one an elegant rectangular fitted box, the other a two-tiered oval box with a wire frame holding the bottle upright. It was made until the early 1950s, as was *Madrigal* (Figure 162), created in 1935. This elaborate ovoid flacon of frosted glass is perched on a pedestal foot and has a long beaded neck terminating in a wide rim topped by a high button stopper. It, too, features dancing maidens, but these are clad in classical robes that cling to their bodies, and they bear aloft long, rippling scarves. It is also known as *Amphore.*

Les Îles d'Or (Figure 163), launched in 1929, was a popular model for Molinard. It lives on

zigzag patterns. The box is a golden flattened half-circle with two small supports holding this magical bottle. A 1949 Molinard publication, issued in honor of its centennial, declared: "Lalique . . . has surpassed himself in designing an ensemble in which the light, the crystal, and the perfume form a perfect union."[19] The bottle was still receiving accolades some ten years after it won a special prize at the 1939 World's Fair in New York.

In 1929, *Calendal* (Figure 161), known also as *Bacchantes* and *Habanita,* was introduced, its ovoid form decorated all around with a frieze of nude women against a floral ground, its high button stopper a mass of tiny stylized blossoms. The warm flowery scent was, according to the 1949 Molinard catalog, as "burning and captivating" as Frédéric Mistral's 1867 novel about a Provençal fisherman, which inspired it. The motif is similar to that on Lalique's vase *Bac-*

Les Îles d'Or created for Molinard in 1929 and produced until the early 1950s. Signed "Lalique" postwar. Also reissued in 1980s with new mold as *Molinard de Molinard* and signed "Creation Lalique." *Figure 163. M-4, M-103*

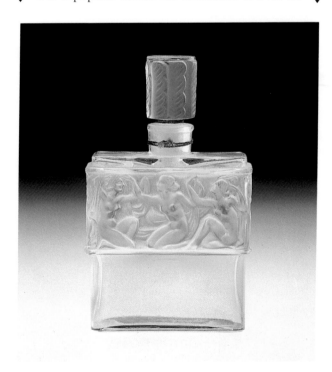

Cariatides was the first and least-known Lalique design for Molinard. Six-faceted flask with floral border design and caryatids. 1928. *Figure 164. M-5*

Three commercial bottles by René Lalique in the 1920s. Left: *Orchis* for Colgate, with a frosted bouquet design. Center: *Semis des Fleurs* for D'Heraud with indented flowers design similar to that in Figure 158. Right: *Le Temps de Lilas* for Houbigant, with stylized design on oval flask. *Figure 165. Col-1, DH-10, H-2*

described in Chapter 2. Throughout its early connections with Napoleons I and III, with Queen Victoria, and with the Czar of Russia at the end of the nineteenth century, the House of Houbigant continued to grow, and in the 1920s it still had a firm hold on the French perfume industry. Its association with Lalique began (and probably ended) in this decade. One of his first designs was *Le Temps de Lilas* (Figure 165), an ovoid flask simply molded with three horizontal rows of neoclassical volutes intersected by vertical reeds. The perfume was introduced to the United States by 1922, when it appeared in various advertisements. *La Belle Saison* (Figure 166), launched in the United States in 1926, is a rectangular flask, molded with an array of radiating leaves framing the lovely profile of a young woman, the flowers entwined in her upswept hair also dotting the perimeter of the bottle. The whole is heavily covered with a brown *patine* and topped by a stopper with a similar leaf and floral

still, its basic all-around frieze of kneeling female nudes who hold swags of cloth appearing on its 1980s reintroduction (containing the scent Molinard de Molinard) as well as on its tall, pinnate-molded stopper. The earliest Lalique flacon for Molinard (1927) was called *Cariatides* (Figure 164) and appears in a Molinard catalog of the 1930s. It is a six-faceted rectangular flask molded with a stylized border and caryatids. *Cariatides* is a simple but striking design and, due to its limited production, is of extreme rarity. Lalique also designed lovely atomizers, or *vaporisateurs,* for Molinard's Le Provençal; these, too, featured friezes of neoclassical female nudes, some in floral or draped settings. A maquette in the same style by Lalique for a Molinard atomizer appears in Figure 73.

Houbigant is another *parfumeur* thriving at the end of the twentieth century, but, unlike Molinard, its roots extend back to the 1700s, as

scents (including Quelques Fleurs and Mon Boudoir), were available in a stunning round box by Lalique, its opalescent-glass cover molded on the inside with a showy and spidery floral (possibly leaf) display, its bottom lined with a cardboard base and overlaid with satin. The charming quartet was nestled in an X-shaped frame. The scents, their bottles, and their wonderful container made for an outstanding presentation—one unique among Lalique's myriad creations.

Volnay, another Parisian *parfumeur,* commissioned Lalique to design bottles for its scents in the 1920s. One, *Gros Fruits—Volnay* (Figure 170), is identical except for its molded name to Maison Lalique's flacon (Figure 54), and two others, *Jasmin du Cap* (Figure 171) and the unnamed square section (Figure 172), are molded with the familiar Lalique design of thorny branches as used in Maison Lalique's *Épines* (Figure 63). *Volnais* (Figure 171), an oval flask with a design of flowering vines, is noteworthy for its

pattern. The perfume was beautifully presented in a green-and-gold leatherlike box (not Lalique's design) embellished with a green tassel and long plastic beads. The similarly shaped *Chypre* (Figure 167) is also known as *Trellis* because of its interweaving design, like that of a wattled fence. Lalique was undoubtedly the designer of the bottle, but an application for a U.S. patent, filed in April 1922, lists Houbigant's Fernand Javal, creator of the scent Idéal (one of the first composite perfumes, in 1900), as its "inventor."

An interesting bottle by Lalique for Houbigant is rather small but significant. Known as the *Triangle Bottle* (Figure 168), because of its three-pointed stopper, the flacon has an open fanlike form. On its own it is lovely but somewhat plain, but as part of the *Ensemble Houbigant* (Figure 169), it comprises a delightful and unique package. Four such bottles, filled with various

The famous 1926 creation *La Belle Saison* for Houbigant. The Art Deco see-through box with tassel adds significantly to the total image. *Figure 166. H-1*

Chypre for Houbigant. Trellis or basketweave design with various stains. 1922. *Figure 167. H-6*

88

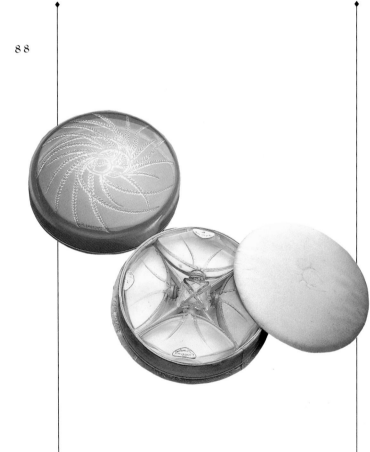

Above: Houbigant standard triangle bottle and variations. Center bottle/stopper used for various Houbigant perfumes and in *Ensemble Houbigant* (Figure 169). Bottles on left and right illustrate two other triangle bottle designs and three other rare stoppers. 1920s. *Figure 168. H-5, H-4, H-5*

Left: *Ensemble Houbigant*, an elegant set of four perfumes in the original opalescent Lalique box. The Houbigant triangular bottles were used for many fragrances. 1920s. *Figure 169. H-3*

Right: *Gros Fruits—Volnay*. Same as Maison Lalique *Gros Fruits* (Figure 54) except with "Volnay Paris" in the mold. 1912–14. *Figure 170. Vo-1*

similarly molded conical stopper, and *Gri-Gri* (Figure 173) is quite unusual, its heart-shaped body and tall thimble stopper molded with a pattern of compressed coral (quite different from Forvil's *Corail Rouge,* Figure 144, and looking more ventricular than coralloid). A 1922 American advertisement for "Les Parfums de Volnay" stated that "Most of Volnay's containers have been designed by the celebrated French artist and jeweler R. Lalique. Every one is a real 'Objet d'Art.' "[20]

Other customers in the prewar period commissioned far fewer bottles from Lalique than those reviewed previously—indeed, a single example is the norm—but several of these are quite noteworthy, not only for their unique designs, but also for the fact that the commissioner was foreign and also not a *parfumeur* at all, but a popular, though "exclusive," department store. Several other fashion houses, too, joined the bandwagon and asked Lalique to design flacons for them.

Madame Gabilla was the first successful woman *parfumeur;* she started out in Paris in the 1890s, creating the scent Mon Chéri in 1910. In the 1920s she commissioned both Baccarat and

Above: Two well-known designs for Volnay from the 1920s. Left: *Jasmin du Cap* is the square flask with the *Épines* motif as in the Maison Lalique model in Figure 63. Right: *Volnais,* with the pointed stopper, has a slightly different decoration with flowers and vines. The stopper is molded "Volnay Paris." *Figure 171. Vo-2, Vo-3*

Above right: Rare square section with *Épines* design for Volnay. Frosted decoration on base and stopper. *Figure 172. Vo-4*

Right: *Gri-Gri* for Volnay is an interesting but unstable heart-shaped flask with a coral decoration. 1921. *Figure 173. Vo-6*

Jardinée is one of the six designs that René Lalique is known to have created for Volnay. The design is of stained flower heads. 1920s. *Figure 174. Vo-5*

Two attractive commercial designs from the 1920s. Left: Pyramid with button stopper for Arys. Stylized flower design with stain. 1920s. Right: *La Violette* for Gabilla with violets design in blue enamel. 1925. *Figure 175. A-11, Gab-1*

Four significant models from the 1920s and '30s. Each with a distinctly different personality. Left to right: *Les Feuillages* for D'Heraud with a tiaralike, two-bird stopper; a cylinder with a dome, name unknown, probably for Maison Lalique; *Imperial* for Lengyal with the Russian double-eagle design; and *Toutes les Fleurs* for Gabilla with the small floral decoration and button stopper. *Figure 176. DH-1, ML-10, Len-1, Gab-2*

Lalique to design flacons for her scents. In 1925 *La Violette* (Figure 175) was launched, an arresting circular flacon molded with a spray of violets tied together at the bottom. The posies themselves are enameled in a blue-violet hue, as are the blossoms on the mushroom top. The stems are clear glass, which gives the flacon an interesting, semiabstract appearance. *Toutes les Fleurs* (Figure 176), which held any one of a number of floral scents (such as Héliotrope, Rose, Pois de Senteur [or Sweet Pea], and Mimosa), has a design of panels of tiny blossoms alternating with plain areas cutting into the ovoid form, giving it a Greek-cross-shaped base. *Lilas* (Figure 80) has a design similar to *Toutes les Fleurs,* but with four arched vaults of petite buds (or *Millefleurs,* as the bottle is also known) giving way to undecorated leaflike forms overhead. *Glycine* (Figure 177) has a cylindrical form narrowing at the bottom and is molded with wisteria blossoms and foliage. It has a blue stain and a stopper molded like knotted rope.

Above left: *Glycine* for Gabilla is an unusual design, a floral motif with a rope-knot stopper. 1920s. *Figure 177. Gab-4*

Above: A dramatic and well-known design by René Lalique, *Bouquet de Faunes,* his only project for Guerlain. Of urn shape with four masks on the shoulders. 1925. *Figure 178. G-1*

Guerlain is another familiar name on the roster of *parfumeurs* for whom Lalique designed flacons, although in the case of this long-established firm only one commission is known. The Picardy-born Pierre-François Guerlain, who had studied both chemistry and medicine in Britain, founded his *parfumerie* in Paris in 1828 on the Rue de Rivoli. In 1848, the shop moved to the smart Rue de la Paix and by the turn of the century, with Guerlain's two sons at the helm, the House of Guerlain was hugely successful, with clients ranging from European royalty to the wives of American *nouveau riches*. Baccarat is the glass house most closely allied with Guerlain; in 1921 it executed the elaborate flacon for the still hugely successful Shalimar scent from a design by Raymond Guerlain, who had been inspired by a piece of antique silver. This was preceded and followed by numerous usually elaborate crystal designs. Lalique's 1924 flacon, too, is quite ambitious: *Bouquet de Faunes* (Figure 178), also known as *Guernais*, came in three sizes and

was in the shape of a classical urn on a pedestal. Its shoulders were molded with four masks, two of satyrs, two of nymphs,[21] and, according to a 1924 American advertisement, it was packaged in a "handsome leather gift case." But the name Lalique appears neither in advertisements nor on the piece itself. It is undoubtedly of the master's design, however, and one can speculate that the esteemed House of Guerlain did not want another well-known name appearing next to its own (it did not publicize the Baccarat name either).

Founded in 1774 and one of the nineteenth century's top *parfumeurs,* L. T. Piver was another client for whom Lalique designed a bottle. This held the scent Misti (Figure 179), but the bottle was also known as *Papillons,* (butterflies) because of its stained butterflies design. Hand-painted butterflies also appear on the soft blue box with "Misti L. T. Piver Paris" placed discreetly in the left-hand corner. Piver, which today is part of Rhône-Poulenc (France) and exports many traditional, fairly heavy scents to the Middle East and other parts of the Third World, commissioned Baccarat to design many of its bottles; these usually were geometric forms, such as the hexagonal form given to their version of *Misti,* which had ornate gilt trim and was introduced

Left: An attractive butterflies design for *Misti* perfume by L. T. Piver. 1923. *Figure 179. P-1*

Below: *Sur Deux Notes,* an oval Art Deco presentation for Renaud. Molded "Lalique." Also a larger size of identical design, shape, and decoration with "RL" and "Lubin" molded in base. Apparently made prewar for Lubin and during and/or postwar for Renaud. Both extreme rarities. *Figure 180. Rel-1*

to the United States in 1927. Lubin, founded in 1793, commissioned one bottle from Lalique, an oval flask with a leaf design all along the sides and a pointed stopper. Oddly enough, the same bottle reappeared later for the perfume *Sur Deux Notes* by Renaud (Figure 180).

Jean de Parys, a Paris *parfumeur* that had an office in New York in 1925 (it was bought much later by L'Oréal[22]), was gifted with three Lalique designs, all highly desirable today. *Sous le Gui* (Figure 181), meaning "Under the Mistletoe," was of black glass. It had a flattened rectangular bottom surmounted by a gold-leafed dome molded with a mistletoe motif (one used again by Lalique, for a large spherical chandelier and a vase). A long red tassel emerged from the top of the dome. Such an olive-green tassel was featured on *Chypre* (Figure 182). The clear glass

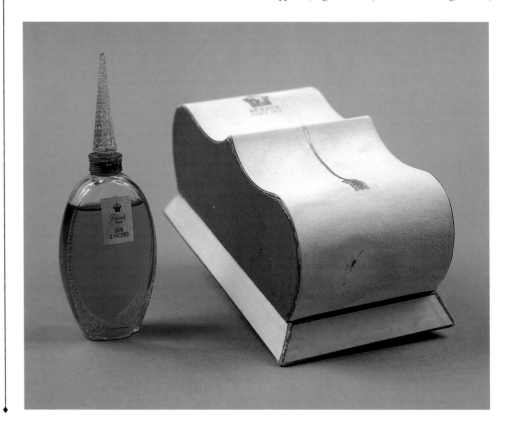

bottle was decorated with a swirling gold enamel plume and boxed in a gold frame to enhance the overall presentation. Both were offered separately or together in a special presentation box (Figure 183).

The other bottle for Jean de Parys was for its scent Premier Désir (Figure 184), of which only one example is known (in the collection of Marie-Claude Lalique). This rare blue-patinated flacon is a mound-shaped piece whose large stopper is in fact a kind of pansy- or violet-covered roof on the wide, squat, cylindrical bottle bottom. It once had a blue tassel emerging from the top, although only a hole is there today. The *parfumeur*'s and scent's names are molded onto the side of the base, and panels of vertical lines embellished with blue *patine* are also on the sides. The interesting thing about this bottle is that its architectonic qualities make it reminiscent of the massive Primavera pavilion at the 1925 Paris Exposition, which had a funnel-shaped dome punctuated by glass lenses by Lalique. Although the roof's design was not floral, it nonetheless bore

Left: The dramatic piece *Sous le Gui* (Under the Mistletoe) for Jean de Parys from the Roaring Twenties era. *Chypre* and *Sous le Gui* were offered separately or in one presentation box. Three known complete with tassel. *Figure 181. JP-2*

Below: Fabulous presentation by René Lalique for *Chypre* by the perfumer Jean de Parys. Only two known complete with box, label, gold enamel, and with tassel intact. 1925. *Figure 182. JP-1*

a resemblance to the florid stopper of *Premier Désir*'s bottle.

Another quintessential Art Deco flacon was designed for Corday of Paris for its scent *Tzigane* (Figure 187), which was touted as being "for the gypsy in your soul" (*tzigane* means gypsy). Corday was a young firm, relatively speaking, having been founded in 1921. Its name derived from Girondist revolutionary Charlotte Corday, who in 1793 killed in his bath Jean-Paul Marat, who had been instrumental in overthrowing the Girondists. Although Corday's signature scent was Toujours Moi, Tzigane was quite popular, if only for its frosted-glass cylindrical bottle molded with a dizzying geometric design of spiraling zigzags. One of Lalique's more moderne creations, its stylization was bold and refreshing (and quite a change from Corday's usual Bac-

93

Left: *Chypre* and *Sous le Gui* for Jean de Parys; in leather presentation case. Only one known set complete. 1929. *Figure 183.* JP-1, JP-2

Right: *Premier Désir* for Jean de Parys with deep blue stain over a floral design. Molded on front "Premier Désir—Jean de Parys." 1920s. *Figure 184. JP-3*

94

Left: Two very rare Art Deco commercial bottles for unknown perfumers. Beading decoration to base and disk stopper of flacon on left. Flared frosted sides with draped design on right. *Figure 185.* UK-6, UK-5

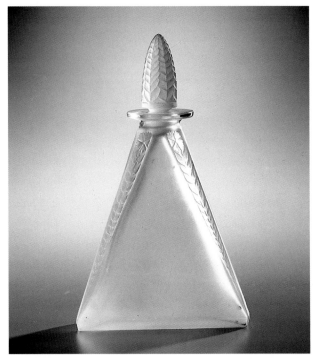

Right: Triangular flask of Art Deco flavor for unknown commercial perfumer. Fern leaf design on sides and pointed stopper. Possibly for Lubin (Figure 180), as decoration is similar. *Figure 186. UK-9*

189 and 190). One had a pagodalike design, its rings touched with black enamel dots and reminiscent of Worth's *Imprudence* (Figure 134). It was presented in a very modern 30s-type box made up of black, white, and silver lines. The other was a square flask and stopper with scalloped edges, the body of the flacon sporting stylized bubbles. This bottle has been seen by the authors only in illustrated advertisements, and from these prints it is not possible to discern whether the bubbles are molded in the glass, applied as enamel, or even trapped within the glass. If the latter is true, then the bottle may not be Lalique's design, even though advertisements in the mid-1930s claimed this.

Parfums Lionceau, at 110 Rue Demours in Paris, filled its one Lalique-designed flacon—*Pierre Précieuse* (Figure 191), also known as *Diamont* because its gold-enameled body was dotted at the center with a glass "diamond"—with thir-

carat-made flacons, which were traditionally shaped and molded). Even its box, not designed by Lalique, was a stunner: pink satin-covered cardboard in the form of a violin.

Another strong stylized design covered both the box and flacon of *Canarina* (Figure 188). The frosted blue glass bottle has a simple square shape with a flat square stopper, but molded all over on one side are eleven stylized eyes. The same Egyptian-style almond eyes appear on the perfume's embossed cardboard box. Lalique might well have been inspired by the 1922 discovery of Tutankhamen's tomb in Egypt—which spurred on an Egyptian revival in the Art Deco era—when he designed this lovely piece.

Lalique designed two flacons for Delettrez of Paris in the 1930s for its *Inalda* scent (Figures

An Art Deco design, *Tzigane*, for Corday, along with a Lalique shop display sign for D'Orsay. *Tzigane* was the only Lalique flacon for Corday and it came in five sizes 1930. *Figure 187. Cor-1*

Clever Art Deco design for Canarina's *"Les Yeux Bleus."* Blue glass with white stain on "eyes" design. 1920s. *Figure 188. Can-1*

Announcement / advertise-
ment for *Inalda* by Delettrez. Both bottles are very
scarce. Black-enamel dots on
rings of circular model on
right, which is also shown in
Figure 190 with its original
box. *Figure 189. Del-2,
Del-1*

The tiered cylindrical bottle
Inalda for Delettrez, com-
plete with its original box.
Art Deco presentation of sil-
ver and black. 1934. Rare.
Figure 190. Del-1

teen of its scents (including Parfum pour
Blondes, Parfum pour Brunes, Lune de Venise,
and Poème Arabe). Still, despite its many possible contents, the flacon is one of the rarest
today. Its extremely elegant three-tiered leatherette black box is embossed with multicolored
flowers. The name *Pierre Précieuse* appears on the
inside tier, which can be lifted out and propped
up to better display the *diamont* bottle.

An unusual 1936 bottle contained Lengyel's
Parfum *Impérial* (Figure 176). Atypical for its traditional design, the ovoid flask was molded with
the Russian double-eagle motif, the crown of
Empress Catherine forming its stopper. Lengyel
was a Parisian *maître-parfumeur,* not Russian, but
it is interesting to inject here the hypothesis that
there may have been a connection between Imperial Russia and René Lalique. The Rallet firm,
which was (and still is) one of the most important manufacturers worldwide of raw materials,
or essences, for perfumes, had a branch in Moscow in the early twentieth century. The Chiris

rectangular flask from René Lalique for its scent *Chose Promise* (Figure 193), but with an interesting stopper, a very tall rectangular piece molded with a draped female nude. Although no other Fioret flacons have come to light, it should be mentioned that the boxes of some of the firm's fragrances were distinguished by the circular glass pendants by René Lalique that embellished them (Figure 194). They were pierced with three holes—two at the top, one below—through which silk ribbon was hung and knotted, the bottom knot ending in a fringed tassel. Pendants such as these are highly collectible today.

Only one Lalique design was executed for Lalo of Paris, for its perfume *Auteuil* (Figure 195). The squat globular flacon was molded all over with a petal motif; the stopper was a flattened button-type flower head. Only three of these are known, making it a very rare Lalique bottle.

In 1928, Veolay *parfumerie* of Paris advertised a heart-shaped bottle for its *Niobe Violet*

97

family of Grasse was a co-owner of the Rallet firm, but in 1916 the Bolsheviks seized the company and the Chirises lost their ownership (although they formed another firm, the present-day Rallet/France). François Carnot, mentioned earlier as president of the Union Centrale des Arts Décoratifs and the acquaintance of both Lalique and François Coty, was one of the directors of Rallet Moscow (as well as married to a member of the Chiris family). He may well have asked René Lalique to design a flacon for the Russian Rallet company before the Revolution, but as yet no Russian bottle signed "R. Lalique" has been found.[23] A Lalique bottle for Rallet/France is shown in figure 192.

Fioret of Paris commissioned a rather simple

Pierre Précieuse, a very unusual gold enameled flacon for Lionceau with "diamond" inset and leatherette box. Available with choice of thirteen different perfumes. 1924. One known with original box. *Figure 191. Lio-1*

Frosted design of nude and satyr on simple, but elegant, square flask. Made for *Soir Antique* perfume by Rallet. *Figure 192. Ra-1*

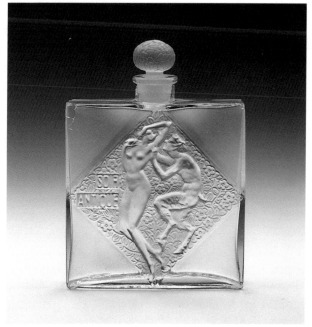

Left: *Chose Promise* for Fioret is a very rare flacon with an unusually tall stopper of a nude female design. Molded and stained "Fioret Paris" and "Chose Promise" on the face of the flask. It is the only known bottle of Lalique design for Fioret, although he created pendants for this client, as illustrated in Figure 194. Probably 1920s. One known complete with original box. *Figure 193. Fio-1*

Right: A pair of Lalique glass pendants for Fioret. Generally these were offered as part of a deluxe fragrance presentation, but not with a Lalique-designed flacon. Only one scent bottle is known to have been designed by Lalique for Fioret —*Chose Promise* (Figure 193). *Figure 194.*

(Figure 196), whose shoulders were molded with two lovebirds amid tree branches. Its attenuated heart-shaped stopper was molded on its thick sides as well with a leafy design. In 1928 this bottle sold for $18.

For de Vigny at least three Lalique bottles from the 1920s exist: one, in the collection of Marie-Claude Lalique, is a sharply tapering cylinder with a long, pointed stopper, for the scent *L'Ambre de Vigny* (Figure 197). It is noteworthy for its resemblance to a Lalique carafe, namely, *Marguerites Bouchon Pointe* (see 1932 catalog, plate 97, number 3161), the daisies covering the stopper entirely and trailing down the body in four regular molded streams. For de Vigny's now-rare *D'où Vient'il* (Figure 198), Lalique chose a molded butterflies design. Other French *parfumeurs* for whom Lalique designed at least one flacon—and about whom little is known today—include Alpy (Figure 31), Anna (Figure

Right: A rare and well-designed bottle for *Auteuil*, a scent for Lalo. Apparently this was the only Lalique flacon for this firm. One known complete with original box. *Figure 195. Lal-1*

98

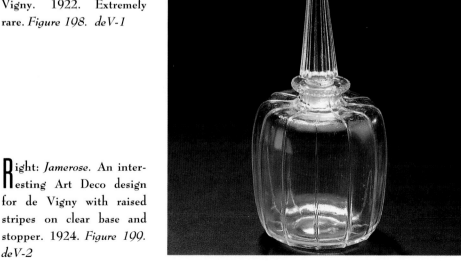

Left: The only known Lalique design for Veolay, *Niobe Violet*. Bird images applied to the shoulders of the bottle. 1928.
Figure 196. Veo-1

Right: Very rare *L'Ambre* for de Vigny. Same design as carafe *Marguerites Bouchon Pointe*, 1932 Lalique catalog, plate 97, number 3161. *Figure 197. deV-3*

Left: A beautiful butterfly stopper tops the triangular flask *D'où Vient'il* for de Vigny. 1922. Extremely rare. *Figure 198. deV-1*

Right: *Jamerose*. An interesting Art Deco design for de Vigny with raised stripes on clear base and stopper. 1924. *Figure 199. deV-2*

217), and Erasmic (Figure 200), for which he designed a circular flask with a woman between two butterflies, as opposed to the female-butterfly hybrid for D'Heraud's *Phalène* (Figure 152), wherein a woman's body wears the insect wings. Tokalon's *Petalia* (Figure 201), also known as *Captivant de Tokalon,* is very rare today; it sports a stunning sunburst face. This solar motif was quite popular in the Art Deco period and derived from Egyptian representations of the god Aten's sun disk. In the 1920s and 30s, however, the design was highly stylized and half-suns or whole orbs were usually depicted in a surround of glorious angled rays of light.

A Lalique bottle was presented by the Parisian *grand magasin* (department store) Galeries Lafayette, but *La Feuillaison* (Figure 24) was just a Lalique Coty bottle, *Muguet* (Figure 29), with a different stopper and label. Also in this vein, Louvre's Öeillet bottle (*öeillet* means carnation) was identical to Coty's *Lipas Pourpre* (Figure 32), but with a different label, and Louvre's *Danae* and Claire's *Orée* bottles (Figure 202) are quite similar except for their labels and the fact that

Three highly styled flasks that reflect many of the strong aspects of the early Art Deco style. The two examples on either side were probably commercial bottles for unknown perfumes. The leaves and flowers on the circular flask are beautifully accented by the black stain. The oval example on the right with the pointed stopper has frosted bands of birds and berries. The center bottle was for the Erasmic company, perfume unknown. It bears the stain-enhanced motif of a lady between two butterflies. It is molded "Erasmic" on the stopper. All probably early 1920s and extremely rare. *Figure 200. UK-3, Era-1, UK-4*

one depicts a draped maiden while the other has her nude. In fact, all these Lalique flacons seem to be Coty promotional products made especially for European and American department stores, under different names and with different labels. These included John Wanamaker's in Philadelphia (for whom Lalique provided interior decoration around 1932, including massive figurative panels of sandblasted glass), the abovementioned Louvre store (not connected with the museum) and Le Printemps in Paris, Bloomingdale's in New York, and Harrods in London. Indeed, in the Cristal Lalique archives in Paris is a 1914 René Lalique drawing for Coty's Meteor scent bearing the ornamental words "Meteor/Harrods/London." No bottle has been found bearing this label and the scent itself was not marketed in the United States until the late 1940s. Likewise, a label for Coty's Styx fragrance, for the Parisian department store Le Printemps is in the Crystal Lalique files.[24]

An interesting connection can be made between Lalique and the Institut de Beauté, for whom he created the flacon *Klytia* (Figure 208) with its stylized wave design. The elegant beauty salon, whose proprietor was Victor Merle, was located at 26 Place Vendôme, on the upper floors of the address right next to Lalique's at number 24 (the fine jeweler Boucheron was and still is on the ground floor).[25] No doubt one reason Lalique took the beauty shop as a client was its proximity to his establishment; no other such business is among those who commissioned him to design their flacons.

The House of Gal was a Spanish fragrance firm for whom Lalique designed one bottle in 1925, for *Gal-Madrid* (Figure 209), with a stained leaf design. Besides the Dutch shipping firm, Rotterdam Lloyd, whose limited-edition Royal Dutch Mail-labeled scent was packaged in the *Cactus* flacon, all Lalique's other clients seem to have been French or American.

Lalique's American commissions were quite small in number, but three are quite significant. The exclusive New York fashion salon Jay-

Below left: The molded sunburst face decoration of *Petalia* for Tokalon is most striking. 1925. Only three known, one complete with box. *Figure 201. To-1*

Below: Two Lalique commercial bottles for Coty department-store promotions in the mid-1920s. Bottles almost identical except that figure is draped in one version and nude in the other. Left to right: Louvre and Claire are the department stores and *Danae* and *Orée*, respectively, are the Coty Perfumes. *Figure 202. Lu-1, Cl-1*

Thorpe Co., commissioned one bottle from Lalique, for its scent bottle *Jaytho* (Figure 210), subtitled *Méchant Mais Charmant* (meaning "Naughty But Nice"), which was introduced in 1927. An advertisement from that year featured a drawing of Lalique's *Crystal Flacon* in a geometric setting. Its oval, frosted glass body is molded all over with a high-relief design of tulip blossoms, and its stopper is in the shape of a tulip bud. "Jaytho" is molded on the bottom middle bud and the whole is highlighted with a green *patine*. Two larger bottles and a matching box were also produced, though probably not all made by Lalique as most are not signed. Jay-Thorpe is notable, too, for commissioning Lalique to decorate part of the interior of its Fifty-seventh Street showroom. Around 1928 he completed designs for the entrance salon and so-called Crystal Room of the Jay-Thorpe Building.

The Alexander and Oviatt department store

Left: Slender pyramid in carafe style. Eau de Toilette *Oree* for Claire. Daisies design on the disk stopper. *Figure 203. Cl-2*

Right: *La Sirène* is a distinctive and extremely rare Lalique creation for Burmann. Concave center with mermaid design. A larger example, probably experimental, is shown in Figure 218 with a different stopper and a modified mermaid pose. *Figure 204. Bur-1*

Left: *Vinca*, an extremely rare and striking Art Deco design of black-enamel squares over frosted body, for Coryse. Circa 1928. *Figure 205. Cse-1*

Right: A simple, clean design for an unknown commercial perfume, usually called *Lierre*. Floral stopper. *Figure 206. UK-1*

Left: Clever rectangular compartments with separate bird-design stoppers. Probably commercial bottle for unknown perfumer. One known. *Figure 207.* UK-2

Right: *Klytia.* A very rare Art Deco design of the early 1930s for Institut de Beauté (Beauty Salon) located on the upper floor of the Place Vendôme shop next door to Lalique's. *Figure 208.* IB-1

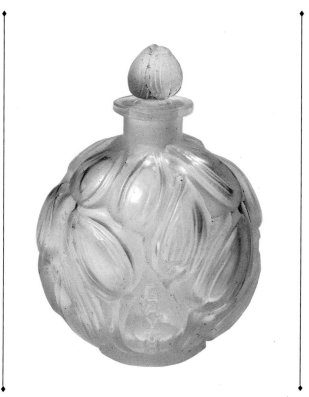

Left: An attractive model for the House of Gal, Madrid. Stylized leaf design. 1925. *Figure 209.* Gal-1

Right: *Méchant Mais Charmant* with a tulips design for Jay-Thorpe Co., a New York fashion salon in the 1920s and 30s. "Jaytho" molded on face of bottle. Also, two larger-size bottles of identical design (except for clear band in middle) usually without Lalique signature. *Figure 210.* JT-1

in Los Angeles was another customer of Lalique's. Not only did he design architectural pieces for this establishment, but he also provided the store with a perfume bottle for its scent Le Parfum des Anges (The Perfume of the Angels being an appropriate name for a scent in the City of the Angels), which was created for the opening of the Oviatt Building in 1927. This bell-shaped bottle (Figure 211) has a stopper in the shape of a clover, and its body (frosted for perfume, clear for eau de cologne) is molded with two mirror-image angels holding on to a large bell, their wings forming a circular headdress in the background (this basic design is also that of the seal of the City of Los Angeles). The fragrance's name runs around the shoulder of most of the bottles, whereas others lack the name and sport a cylindrical metal stopper. A cardboard container for the bottle was embossed with the same angelic image, cameo colored on a silver-gray ground. The French *parfumeur* Worth is supposed to have provided Oviatt with the scent for *Le Parfum des Anges*.

Another New York department store, Saks Fifth Avenue, commissioned Lalique to design a

A special commission perfume bottle for the opening of the Oviatt Building in Los Angeles in 1927. Design includes the seal of the City of Los Angeles and the perfume name, *Le Parfum des Anges*. The building, which is on the Historical Register, also contains architectural pieces of René Lalique's design. Available in clear and charcoal gray. *Figure 211. O-1*

A store display sign by Lalique for Miro Dena, a Paris and New York perfumer of the 1920s and 30s. A strikingly similar motif to the Coty design in Figure 19. Molded "R. Lalique." There is no evidence that Lalique designed any flacons for Miro Dena. *Figure 212.*

very special flacon for them, which they featured in an exhibition of Lalique's works (*garnitures de toilette* and other glass pieces) held in the store in 1939. Only fifty were produced (to commemorate Saks' golden jubilee being celebrated that year) and, true to its name, *Trésor de la Mer* (Figures 213 and 214) is a unique treasure to behold. The flacon is molded and finished to make it look like a satiny pearl, and it comes in a lovely box molded as a frosted and opalescent oyster shell on a bed of frothy waves. It has only recently come to light among collectors that this box (which was known for a long time by its alternate name, *Mollusque*) contained a pearl flacon within; so far only one such complete treasure-in-the-oyster set has been seen, and this was displayed in a Lalique and Cristal Lalique exhibition held by Saks Fifth Avenue in late 1987.

Magnum Import Company of New York largely repackaged French perfumes and sold them to the American market, their offerings including a variety of Caron and Coty scents. At least three examples of the Lalique-designed purse-size flacon are known (Figure 215). Colgate, the massive conglomerate founded in the late nineteenth century and located in New Jersey, commissioned a single bottle from Lalique, for its *Orchis* scent (Figure 165). It has a molded floral design and, compared to most of the firm's

bottles—quite plain in the 1920s, although they would be liberally embellished in the Belle Époque—it was relatively elaborate, though not significant in terms of Lalique's own *oeuvre*. The orchid design also appears at the top of the box with lavender and black lines running outward.

The final group of prewar *parfumeurs* to whom Lalique lent a designing hand is composed of French couturiers, all of whom, as has been mentioned before, were eager to jump on the bandwagon and market a "house scent" or two, or even a larger range of products. Foremost of these was Lucien Lelong, whose father had owned a textiles shop where Lucien learned about fabrics and who in 1914, at the age of twenty-four, presented his first collection of ball gowns. After serving in World War I, Lelong opened a couture house on the Place de Madeleine and remained hugely successful for decades, employing, among others, Pierre Balmain, Christian Dior, and Hubert de Givenchy before

Two views of the exquisite *Trésor de la Mer* for Saks Fifth Avenue. Limited edition of fifty made for the 1939 Lalique Exhibition at Saks on the occasion of Saks' fiftieth anniversary. Opalescent shell box with pearl-shaped perfume insert. Only one complete set known. *Figures 213 and 214. Saks-1*

Magnum was a New York importer who repackaged various perfumes, including Coty and Caron brands, in this unusual purse-size vial. 1920s. *Figure 215. Mag-1*

Left: Unusual design, probably for a commercial perfumer, with overlapping petal design. Extremely rare. *Figure* 216. UK-8

Right: A simple Art Deco design with unusual tiered stopper for Anna. Stopper reminiscent of *Imprudence* for Worth. 1927. Very rare. *Figure 217. An-1*

they went on to found their own *maisons*. In 1924 Lelong established the Société des Parfums Lucien Lelong, calling his first four scents, simply but intriguingly, A, B, C, and N (the latter possibly after Princess Nathalie Paley, his second wife). His *parfumerie* flourished, as did his couture house, with Lelong himself designing many of his scents' containers.[26] René Lalique created two Lelong flacons, however, and they number among his most moderne. Around 1938 a stunning bottle (Figure 129) with matching metal case was designed by Lalique and contained the four aforementioned lettered scents plus another one, J.[27] Probably intended for the American market, the stylish square-section bottle, with a complementary squared-off stopper, was of frosted glass enameled in either black or brown with tiers of simple swags, an elegant fish-scale-like motif. Its matching box (with opposing color scheme, however, from the flacons, the

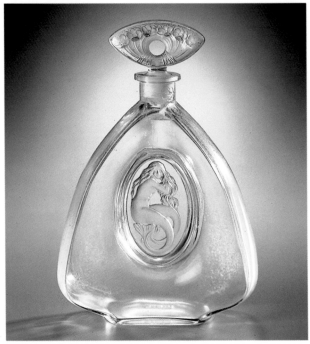

Right: A larger version of Burmann's *La Sirène* (Figure 204) with different stopper and mermaid in slightly different pose. Probably the eau de toilette size or an experimental model. *Figure 218.*

106

color being on the body, not the fillips) was also of black- or brown-enameled metal highlighted with silvered-metal swags—this time two large rows on its body, another pair on its two-stepped, wedding-cake-like tiered stopper. The swags, in fact, bear a resemblance to the pearly garlands of *Palerme* (Figure 37) and *Perles* (Figure 26) and to some of the elegant decoration on furniture of the Art Deco period (although Lelong's swags may, of course, be an appropriate reference to flowing drapery, as Lelong's own Brosse-made bottle design for his scent *Indiscrèt* was several years later). It is no surprise that this architectonic masterpiece is also known as *Skyscraper,* especially as its black and silver box mimics materials prevalent in moderne urban-American buildings—that is, chromium, nickel, Monel, and other shiny metals, which were often coupled with black marble or granite. Also for Lelong's scents Lalique designed the *Étoile de*

Four Art Deco flacons for various perfumers. Left to right: *Bigarade* for Nina Ricci, an oval cylinder with ribs and a gold screw-on stopper. 1945–50. Two presentations for Arys, *Premier Oui* and *Un Jour Viendra.* The latter is the larger size of the version in Figure 121. Both 1919. *Étoile de Mer,* an octagonal fluted cylinder for Lucien Lelong. 1931.
Figure 219. NR-115, A-2, A-9, LL-2

Mer (Figure 219) flacon, a smart, octagonal fluted cylinder available in two sizes. Meaning "starfish," the bottle was in fact in the shape of an eight-pointed multilayered star (starfish usually have five arms, not eight), as was its matching stopper. The final result was chic and moderne, however with no nautical connotations whatsoever except for its name.

Martial et Armand was an exclusive French couture house located at both 13 Rue de la Paix and 10 Place Vendôme during the 1920s (in fact, one of its scents was named Place Vendôme). Lalique's sole design for Martial et Armand (Figure 220), from 1926, was eponymously named, but also known as *Un Rien,* another of the firm's scents. Its flattened ovoid flask body, straight at the bottom, was molded with two female heads outlandishly coiffed in what appear to be Louis XV–style powdered and beaded wigs, but these so stylized as to almost resemble the furry black

108

Left: A design of coiffed females in the Louis XV style for the couturier Martial et Armand, neighbor of Lalique on the Rue de la Paix, just off the Place Vendôme. Various perfumes used in the presentation, including Un Rien. 1926. *Figure 220. M&A-1*

Right: Art Deco double-square design for Molyneux. Frosted interlocking squares design. 1926. *Figure 221. Mol-1*

bearskin helmets of the guards at Buckingham Palace. The two hairstyles in effect form a letter *V* and are surrounded by both a frosted-glass heart shape (cut off at the bottom, like the bottle itself) and a large partial *M* at the left and partial *D* at the right, the first and last letters of the fashion house's name, which appears in stylized —and very moderne—uppercase characters on the level of the two ladies' chins. The stopper is in the form of a heart as well, although it is actually the letter *M* with a large *A* entwining it. The flacon, in five sizes, two with slightly different, more attenuated shapes, held, besides Un Rien, the scents Place Vendôme, Chypre, and Ambre.

For the British-born couturier Edward Molyneux (1891–1974), who began marketing scents by the 1930s, Lalique is known to have designed at least one flacon in two sizes, this a rectilinear shape comprising two interlocking squares (Figure 221). J. F. Davy of Roger et Gallet recollects that Lalique designed at least one other flacon for Molyneux, this molded on its

Right: *L'Île d'Amour*—a vanity set —was introduced by Lournay in 1921 as a one-time special offer. The advertisement states: "Bottles of hand-wrought glass, encrusted with copper, the work of Lalique, famous artist of France. No second set will be made from this design. The case is of suede. Price $500." A heady price for 1921. *Figure 222. Lor-1*

rectangular body with top and bottom borders and a central heart made up of daisies *(marguerites),* with a small tiara-type stopper.[28] An actual bottle has not been located, however.

Vintage periodicals and other more recent sources have named Lalique as the designer of other *parfumeries'* flacons, including Rigaud, Clamy, Marny, Lenthéric, Eliane, Arly, Luyties, and Richard Hudnut, but these have not been confirmed. Indeed, many such candidates clearly do not manifest the master's distinctive touch in either their actual designs or their molding or method of production. Some may indeed be signed "R. Lalique" or "Lalique" (after René's death the "R." was dropped on the signature, although some of the earliest bottles were signed without the "R."), but they may have had a signature added to them later, even though the bottle was made in the 1920s or 30s. On the other hand, Lalique records suggest that he may have executed at least one example for Grenoville, Khourie, and Vassco as well as one or two additional scent bottles for Worth, Arys, Forvil, Colgate, Houbigant, Jean de Parys, and Molinard.

Above left: Dramatic octagonal flask for unknown commercial perfumer. Black enamel Art Deco design of stylized flowers.
Figure 223. UK-7

Above: *A Travers la Voilette,* for Isabey. Simple square flask decorated with flower and leaf design in black and gold enamel. (Decoration signed "Alix.")
Figure 224. Is-1

Right: A treasured bottle for Raquel Meller. Enameled on both sides with orange flower blossoms on black background. Signature intaglio. *Figure 225. RM-1*

CHAPTER 5

Postwar to the Present

THE FLACONS DESCRIBED IN CHAPTERS 3 AND 4 comprise the vast majority of Lalique perfume bottles, but a large and significant body of Cristal Lalique glass works followed the death of René Lalique in 1945.

A total of thirty-five scent bottles are known to have been designed and introduced under the direction of Marc Lalique or his daughter Marie-Claude Lalique. Nine were for Cristal Lalique direct sales to the public (seven of which are currently manufactured) and the balance for commercial perfume companies (more than half for Nina Ricci).

The master's demise more or less coincided with the liberation of Alsace and the start of the renovation of the Wingen-sur-Moder factory, which had been damaged in the war. There had been sparse production during the hostilities with only the Combs-la-Ville glassworks available, since in 1940 the Wingen facilities were shut down and the area occupied by the Germans for the rest of the war.

When the Wingen-sur-Moder factory was reopened Marc Lalique began manufacturing prewar designs of his father's as well as some of

Left: One of Marc Lalique's first designs, the unusual *Requête* for Worth, with blue enamel. Designed late 1944. *Figure 226. W-105*

Above: The post-1952 version of *Imprudence* for Worth with the Marc Lalique stopper for easier opening. *Figure 227. W-107*

his own creations. Marc Lalique, whose technical knowledge and engineering skills had served him and the firm well when he was the plant manager and head administrator, introduced a new higher-lead glass mixture as well, turning the company's output from *demi-cristal* into a sleek, crisp, *moderne cristal*. He also largely eliminated colored glass and colored staining or enamel applications to glass and decreased the production of opalescent glass, finally ceasing it, too, in the 1950s.

Cristal Lalique's flacons and those created for commercial perfumes include some that are as rare and collectible as earlier René Lalique designs. One of these is for Worth's *Requête* (Figure 226), a sophisticated round flask edged all around with a strong scalloped design, this highlighted in blue enamel, one of the few works with applied color created by Marc Lalique. Blue enamel also goes around the rim of the bottle's tall neck and on the three concentric rings molded on the stopper, which is monogrammed on the top with a "W" and has an inverted conical shape, like a Russian cossack's hat. Worth introduced the scent, its first since the war began, around

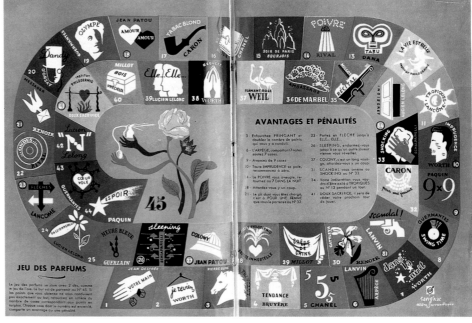

Above left: *Le Voyageur* was a purse-size flask for Worth that came complete with a suede pouch. Early 1950s. *Figure 228. W-102*

Above: An unusual parlor board, *Jeu des Parfums* (Game of Perfumes), apparently from the 1940s. Most of the major perfume houses of the period are represented. *Figure 229.*

Left: A rare war era creation by Marc Lalique, *Marrakech*, for Lancôme. Clear with flared sides. 1946. *Figure 230. Lan-104*

1945, and, contrary to earlier beliefs that René Lalique designed the flacon in the late 1930s but that it was not produced until after his death, Worth has confirmed that it is undoubtedly a Marc Lalique creation.[1]

As mentioned earlier in the discussion on Worth, the René Lalique bottles for Dans la Nuit, Je Reviens, Imprudence, and Sans Adieu were made after World War II and into the 1950s with variations such as altered stoppers as well as the deletion of the "R." in the signature. More recently, in 1985, the *Dans la Nuit* sphere with stars and the cobalt blue flask have been reintroduced and are marked "Creation Lalique."

In 1946 Marc Lalique designed a perfume bottle for Lancôme called *Marrakech* (Figure 230). The flacon was in the shape of a vase or carafe with an upward flared design on the sides, the perfume contained in the center. It bore the "Lalique" molded signature in contrast to the unsigned later examples for Lancôme.

In the next decade, circa 1952, three addi-

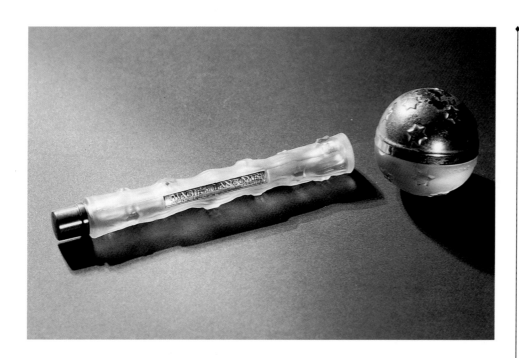

 amples in the 1940s. *Femme* (Figure 233) has been available for many years, although it appears that only the early examples were signed. The other model, *La Rose* (Figure 234), is more rare, but the design and size were altered and it was reintroduced as the Cristal Lalique presentation *Moulin Rouge*. The concave floral center motif is its outstanding feature.

The lovely flacon designed for Morabito's *No. 7* scent (Figure 135), 1951, has often been identified as a René Lalique design, although we tend to believe it was a Marc Lalique creation; in any event it was definitely introduced after the war. Also known as *Tortues (Tortoises),* the spherical amber-orange glass flacon has a body comprising the stylized shells of four turtles, their heads angled up to form the neck, and perched atop a wide disk rim is a bulbous stopper, molded with the same hexagonal scaled design as that on the animals' shells. The strong color of the glass provides an argument in favor of the René Lalique attribution, but a July 1951

113

tional designs for Lancôme were introduced. There was *Sphère Magie* (Figure 231), a glass globe dotted with stars (looking very much like the irregular star shapes of the *Amethyst* flacon, Figure 14) and capped on its northern hemisphere with a 14-carat gold-plated dome, and, also for the fragrance Magie, or *Baton de Magicien,* a frosted-glass wand molded with stars on its knobbly, wavy surface and with a metal-plated cylindrical screw cap. Another design for Lancôme was a tiny twin set, *Jumeles* (Figure 232), containing two half-ounce bottles of Magie and Tropiques. The Lancôme firm was founded by onetime Coty employee Armand Petitjean in 1935 and had a roster of royal clients, including Queen Elizabeth II and the late Duchess of Windsor. Magie was launched in France in 1946, but in heavy crystal flacons by Baccarat, packaged in a vivid, sequin-studded white satin jewel box.

Another of Marc Lalique's early clients was Marcel Rochas, for whom he designed two ex-

Two Marc Lalique designs from the early 1950s for Lancôme. Left to right: *Magie,* or *Baton de Magicien,* and *Sphère Magie,* both with star decoration. *Figure 231. Lan-101, Lan-102*

Jumeles, designed by Marc Lalique for Lancôme in the early 1950s. Cylinder bases angled and bodies notched so that the pair stand together. *Figure 232. Lan-103*

entry for Morabito's *Tortoises* in the Cristal Lalique archives weighs heavily against it. René Lalique did in fact design a lovely vase in the 1920s called *Tortues* (see 1932 catalog, plate 17, number 966), of a similar color glass and with a cluster of elaborately molded, convex turtle bodies comprising its globular form. Perhaps Morabito's flacon was a deliberate effort on Marc Lalique's part to pay homage to, but tone down and modernize at the same time, his father's far more elaborate and complex design.

Raphael of Paris commissioned one item from Lalique, a tiny scent pendant (Figure 148) in the form of an acorn, its gilt-metal cap molded with tiers of graduated fish scales, as was the

glass bottom. Although the scent contained within *Réplique* originated in the 1940s, this unusual little charm was launched in the United States in 1951. It was uniquely presented in a celluloid-topped box with a bright red ribbon inscribed "Raphael Réplique" tied to the gilt-metal cap.

Through the early 1950s, Molinard continued to market the prewar *Calendal, Madrigal,* and *Les Îles d'Or* (Figures 161, 162, and 163) flacons, although with a variety of different scents and without the "R." in the signature (although the molded "R. Lalique" signature on the side of the *Calendal* model could still be found with a sharp eye). Also, it is probable that some of the *Le*

Left: *Femme* and other Marcel Rochas scents were packaged in this creation by Marc Lalique in 1943. It was made by Lalique until the early 1950s, though most examples are not signed. *Figure 233. Ro-101*

Right: One of the two flacons designed for Marcel Rochas by Marc Lalique, *La Rose.* Floral center design and bottle shape very similar to Cristal Lalique pattern *Moulin Rouge* (Figure 253). 1944. *Figure 234. Ro-102*

Baiser du Faune (Figure 160) bottles were made postwar, and since they are clearly signed in the mold "R. Lalique," they are impossible to differentiate from the earlier ones. This model appeared in the 1949 Molinard centennial catalog. In the 1980s, *Molinard de Molinard* was introduced in the *Les Îles d'Or* flacon (made from a new mold) but was differentiated with the signature "Creation Lalique."

Just as the Coty firm was the *parfumeur* with the strongest, most significant links to René Lalique, so has the Nina Ricci company, with Marc and Marie-Claude Lalique as its designers, become identified with the postwar Lalique firm. Nina Ricci (1883–1970) was born Marie Nielli in Turin, Italy, her family moving to France when

For Nina Ricci. Marie-Claude Lalique: *Fleur de Fleurs* (second from left) with blossom intaglio, 1982, and *Nina* (third from right), an asymmetrical veil. 1987. Marc Lalique, left to right: *Capricci*, in cut-glass style, 1961; *Farouche*, with frosted wings, 1974; the famous *L'Air du Temps* doves, 1947; and *Coeur Joie* with open-heart, 1942.
Figure 235. NR-107, NR-109, NR-108, NR-116, NR-113, NR-103

she was twelve years old. She worked as a dressmaker in Monte Carlo and Paris, began designing at twenty-two, and before she was thirty was celebrated as one of Paris's foremost dress designers, opening her own couture house on the Rue des Capucines in 1932 (with the help of her husband, a jeweler whose surname was Ricci). Madame Ricci's son Robert (born in 1905), who had previously had a successful career as an advertising consultant, became a partner in his mother's firm, diversifying and expanding it as well (he died in August 1988). It was he who decided the fashion house should create and market scent, and he developed the first one during the war years, introducing Coeur Joie (Figure 235) in 1942. According to the Nina Ricci firm,

116

Above: Nina Ricci bottles for L'Air du Temps by Marc Lalique. Left: *Soleil,* the first Lalique bottle for L'Air du Temps, 1940s. A sunburst design extending to scalloped edges. Right: *Flacon aux Colombes,* a miniature version of the doves design with a gilt-metal dove stopper and gilt-mesh bottle holder. 1950s. *Figure 236. NR-110, NR-113*

Left: *Coeur Joie* for Nina Ricci is a 1943 design by Marc Lalique. Molded "NR" at the neck. *Figure 237. NR-105*

Right: An early presentation for L'Air du Temps by Marc Lalique. Gold plastic stopper. *Figure 238. NR-111*

Two postwar designs by Marc Lalique for Nina Ricci and one prewar by René Lalique for Worth. Left: *Je Reviens* in the standard blue flask for Worth with the older button stopper. 1924. Center: *L'Air du Temps* for Nina Ricci in the purse-size oval flask with gold enamel. Right: *Farouche* with the long-neck oval flask, originally used for L'Air du Temps. Early 1950s. *Figure 239. W-2, NR-114, NR-112*

All four sizes of *Coeur Joie* for Nina Ricci with the open-heart design are shown along with the one-heart version of Marc Lalique's vial design for the same perfume. 1940s and 50s. *Figure 240. NR-103, NR-106*

Three of the L'Air du Temps famous presentations for Nina Ricci. Introduced 1947 and often called *Flacon aux Colombes. Figure 241. NR-113*

Fille d'Eve for Nina Ricci by Marc Lalique in various designs and sizes. The apple with leaf stopper came in three sizes. The flasks with gold-plated stoppers came in two sizes and the purse versions in one. Early 1950s. *Figure 242. NR-101, NR-102*

the scent was "an exquisitely refined bouquet of
flowers . . . [that] gave expression to [Robert
Ricci's] ideal of womanhood. He wanted it
younger, more unsullied and more tender than
the sensuous stereotypes of the period."[2] The
bottle was designed by Marc Lalique from "an
original idea" by Robert Ricci. *Coeur Joie* has a
rather complex openwork design of a heart surrounded by the bottle itself, which is a scallop-
edged heart molded with tiny florets and leaves.
It rests on a rectangular foot and has a tall button
stopper molded with similar small flowers. The
design is nothing like René Lalique ever produced and ample evidence of Marc Lalique's hold
on the reins of the firm and his desire to "intro-
duce new and innovative 'Lalique' and to avoid
a retrospective design policy."[3]

Marc Lalique also designed the world-
famous doves flacon for *L'Air du Temps* (Figures
235 and 241), also known as *Flacon aux Colombes*,
a floral blend with spicy overtones introduced in
1947. The elegant crystal bottle, its ovoid body
gently fluted and twisting, is topped by a

Multiple sizes for *Coeur
Joie* for Nina Ricci, by
Marc Lalique in the early
1950s, left. Right: *Cologne
d'Heraud* by René Lalique in
the early 1920s. *Figure 243.
NR-104, DH-4*

frosted-glass stopper of two doves in flight. This
ultrafeminine scent is one of the best-selling in
the world; its flacon (one of five for the scent) is
certainly one of the company's most recogniz-
able and is still heavily used in Nina Ricci's advertising, which calls it, simply, "The most
romantic of perfumes." Another kind of ro-
mance is brought to mind in the early 1950s'
frosted apple-shaped flacon, its stopper an off-
center crystal-clear leaf; it contained, appropriately, the scent called *Fille d'Eve* (Daughter of
Eve), Figure 242.

Simpler flacons were designed for Nina
Ricci by Marc Lalique, including a circular flask
with a spherical stopper, both molded near the
edges with a scallop design, the tall neck molded
with the prominent initials "NR" (Figure 243).
This bottle was available in five sizes and held
Coeur Joie. Another Lalique design, this in 1961,
was for the floral-scented *Capricci* (Figure 235),
which was bottled in a globular flacon with an
allover diamond pattern and an octagonal flattened stopper. The look of the crystal-clear fla-

L a l i q u e   P e r f u m e   B o t t l e s

con was very contemporary and had a cut-glass appearance.

Farouche, introduced by Nina Ricci in 1974, was presented in a flacon quite unlike anything René or Marc Lalique had ever designed (Figure 235). Its modified heart shape (actually resembling a kind of crown) has its two side ears of solid crystal, with the scent—a blend of over 100 ingredients that results in a perfume unique to the wearer—held in the central egg-shaped section. A gilt-metal band encloses the neck, and the stopper is a large crystal sphere.

The 1980s has seen the introduction of two major designs by Marie-Claude Lalique for Nina Ricci. In 1982, the complex scent *Fleur de Fleurs,* comprising floral essences such as lily-of-the-valley, jasmine, and hyacinth with a soft, woody foundation, was launched in a Cristal Lalique flacon (Figure 235). This compressed rounded flask is crystal clear, as is its button stopper, and its neck is highlighted by a gilt-metal collar with a floral motif. Its salient feature, however, is the rippling flower head molded off-center to the right in frosted glass. Again, the design is unmistakably contemporary and chic, and the contrast of smooth to rigid, clear to frosted, is strong, creating an arresting, unusual piece.

The latest Marie-Claude Lalique creation for Nina Ricci, launched in 1987, is *Nina* (Figure 235). The ovoid flask has an asymmetrical veil design, the veil highlighted by the frosted glass. The use of a fabric motif was inspired by the couturier origins of Nina Ricci. It clearly indicates a style consistent with the Lalique tradition, but has its own individualistic flair.

Cristal Lalique is a power to be reckoned with in the design world today, having its own shops in Europe, North America, and Japan (and more scheduled to open in the future) and with independent galleries and department-store outlets even more far-flung. The crystal tableware, the statuettes, the vases, jewelry, and other mas-

Garniture de toilette Duncan, originally designed in 1931 for Maison Lalique, now without "R." in signature. Originally four scent sizes with ball stopper as in Figure 50. Marc Lalique redesigned in 1974 with stopper as shown. *Figure 244. CL-106*

Cactus was designed in 1928 as a single perfume bottle for Maison Lalique (Figure 55) and continues currently in the Cristal Lalique offerings as a *garniture de toilette.* The two perfumes are flanked by a powder box and an atomizer. *Figure 245. ML-519, CL-103*

The *garniture de toilette Enfants* was first available in 1930 from Maison Lalique and is still available from Cristal Lalique without "R." in signature. Perfume bottle in center. *Figure 246. ML-609, CL-107*

Garniture de toilette Dahlia, designed in the 1920s and available in both Maison Lalique and today's Cristal Lalique collection, without "R." in signature. Enamel in center. *Figure 247. ML-615, CL-105*

Left: The Maison Lalique/ Cristal Lalique *Hélène* with Grecian maidens panels was a very popular bottle pre- and postwar. The larger version was made with two rows of panels. *Figure 248. ML-2, CL-109*

Right: An illustration of *St. Germain,* designed for Cristal Lalique, as shown in a 1950s company catalog. The eight-sided bottle was discontinued some years ago. *Figure 249. CL-112*

Robinson is a *garniture de toilette* designed by Marc Lalique for Cristal Lalique in 1946. A similar set (Figure 249) was discontinued in recent years, whereas *Robinson* is in current production. *Figure 250. CL-113*

terpieces and baubles in glass—even a tiny crystal top intended to relieve executive stress—are well known and highly coveted, just as they were in the days of René Lalique. Perfume bottles, too, are a part of Cristal Lalique's collection. These include bottles originally designed by René Lalique and sometimes slightly altered by Marc (such as the *Duncan garniture de toilette,* Figure 244, whose stopper the younger Lalique changed to make it easier to handle). The handsome *Cactus* (Figure 245) and *Enfants* (Figure 246), the lovely *Clairefontaine* (Figure 65) and *Dahlia* (Figure 247) are still in production.

Other René Lalique designs were produced by Cristal Lalique but have since been discontinued, including the Grecian maiden cylinder, *Hélène* (Figure 248) and *Rosace Figurines* (Figure 94), which is almost the same as the prewar version (Figure 55) except for the Marc Lalique two-nymph stopper, which is also used on the

In 1956 Marc Lalique designed *Floride,* a *garniture de toilette* for the Cristal Lalique line that is still in the current selection.
Figure 251. CL-111

stemware pattern Roxane. The latter, inspired by an earlier René Lalique drawing, probably for jewelry, is in the possession of Marie-Claude Lalique. Finally, there was *Deux Fleurs* (or *Deux Marguerites,* Figure 79) with its overlapping flower heads and disk stopper highlighted in black enamel bosses, which is related to a 1925 René Lalique design for Forvil, *Les Anémones* (Figure 143).

Nine perfume flacons are known to have been designed and produced by Cristal Lalique from postwar designs by Marc and Marie-Claude Lalique. Two designs by Marc Lalique, *St. Germain* (Figure 249) and *Robinson* (Figure 250), are quite similar cylinders, one with eight facings, the other with sixteen. They were designed in 1946. *Floride* (Figure 251) was designed by Marc in 1956 and has a carafelike presentation with a choice of three colors for accent appliqués. His creation *Martine* (Figure 252) is an urn-

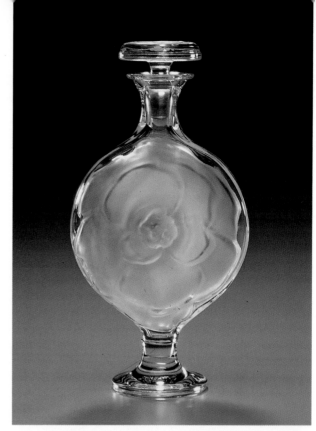

Left: The Cristal Lalique flacon *Martine* is a currently available model designed by Marc Lalique. *Figure 252. CL-114*

Right: *Moulin Rouge* of the present Cristal Lalique line is adapted from *La Rose* for Marcel Rochas, which was designed in 1945 and is shown in Figure 234. *Figure 253. CL-117*

shaped flask with a frosted garland decoration similar to *Robinson*. Marc Lalique's other two Cristal Lalique perfume designs are adaptations of bottles made for Marcel Rochas and Nina Ricci. *Moulin Rouge* (Figure 253) has the same basic design as *La Rose* (Figure 234), except for a slight variation in the floral design, and is 1.6 in (4 cm) shorter. *Pomme* (Figure 254) is basically the same as *Fille d'Eve* (Figure 241), but was reintroduced in the Cristal Lalique collection in one size only in 1976.

Among her many designs for Cristal Lalique, Marie-Claude has created three flacons, the first, *Cassiopée* (Figure 255) in 1963, which shows strong sweeping lines and a complex reflective surface. The other two, *Samoa* (Figure 256) and *Baptiste* (Figure 257), were both introduced in 1979. These have a lighter treatment with swirling designs evoking gracefulness and motion.

Right: The current Cristal Lalique presentation *Pomme* was originally created for Nina Ricci's *Fille d'Eve* in 1952 by Marc Lalique. *Figure 254. CL-116*

Lalique Perfume Bottles

Far left: Marie-Claude Lalique's first *garniture de toilette* for Cristal Lalique was *Cassiopée*, created in 1963. *Figure 255. CL-115*

Left: Marie-Claude Lalique created *Samoa* in 1979. The scent bottle transmits a feeling of motion and gracefulness. The model is currently in production. *Figure 256. CL-118*

Right: *Baptiste* is a Marie-Claude Lalique design from 1979 with an Art Deco spiral motif. The example is in current production. *Figure 257. CL-110*

125

Collecting Lalique
Perfume Bottles

126 RENÉ LALIQUE'S GLASS IS OF MAJOR INTEREST TO collectors today—in Europe, the Americas, Australia, the Middle East, and, ever increasingly, Japan. His and Cristal Lalique's perfume bottles are coveted by the multitude of scent bottle collectors, who consider Lalique's work to be the epitome of design. The market is bipartite (as is the one for Lalique automobile mascots, collected by those interested in Lalique as well as by enthusiasts of vintage automobiles) and therefore quite competitive. A Paris auction of Lalique glass in early 1988 amazed even the experts with the record prices fetched by flacons and related paraphernalia. Even a box full of odd *Dans la Nuit* stoppers garnered a healthy bid!

Over the last ten to fifteen years, the authors' experience has shown that the prices for the prewar, better examples of Lalique perfume bottles have risen more than tenfold. Although prices are not likely to grow at this rate to the turn of the century, the demand certainly gives all indications of strength. Over forty different designs are known to have changed hands in the 1988–89 seasons at prices of $5,000 or more.

But collectors—of both lesser and greater means—need not despair. Lalique created dozens upon dozens of perfume bottle designs in his long career, resulting in, quite literally, millions of bottles, though not all are extant, of course, and his family firm has increased the number quite respectably, so the quantity of flacons is huge. Doubtless thousands of bottles will come out of the closets, drawers, and boudoirs of Europe, America, and elsewhere in the future. There are so many different designs, sizes, and ranges of value that a collector who knows the subject can still find amazing bargains, even in the more sophisticated auction salesroom, not to mention the flea markets, garage sales, and other such venues. Of course, some of the bottles are modestly priced (as low as $30 to $50 because of their sheer abundance coupled with less impressive design), but these may capture someone's fancy nonetheless, if only because of the coveted signature, generally "R. Lalique" before World War II, just plain "Lalique" after the master's death. See the discussion on various signatures in the Appendix.

Of course, with such high demand, the fakes emerge from the attic as well. So far, very

few contemporary René Lalique flacon copies have appeared (although vases and statuettes have), but beware of Lalique-style Art Deco glass being passed off as Lalique. Hastily added engraved or stencil-etched signatures enhance the fakes, but molded signatures are close to impossible to duplicate on an already-made piece of glass, although "applied molded" signatures have been found. Much of this is lesser French glasswork or Czechoslovakian exports. Watch out, too, for signatures trailing down a bottle vertically or appearing too prominently; most of Lalique's flacons were signed fairly discreetly, although his name is not impossible to locate (except on some of his goldwork).

But, signatures aside, it is the look of a piece that should decide whether or not it is "right." A nascent collector can only become a seasoned connoisseur after years of study—not only book study, but actually looking at and feeling the pieces, and talking to the experts about them. Most of the major auction houses in New York, London, and Paris now have sales including or even devoted to Lalique glass. If you can attend one of these, by all means do. Or visit one of the top dealers—Galerie Moderne in London, Nicholas Dawes, Lillian Nassau, Primavera, and

A spectacular lineup of rare and valuable scent bottles included in a London auction July 4, 1980. There were many other outstanding examples in this sale, which attracted worldwide collector attention.
Figure 258.

Renee Antiques in New York, Crystal Galleries in Boulder, Robert Zehil Galleries in Beverly Hills, Danenberg & Cie and Félix Marcilhac in Paris, Kiya Gallery in Tokyo, and Galerie Sanjyo Gion in Kyoto—specializing in Lalique. There are also Régine de Robien (Beauté Divine) in Paris, Madeleine France Antiques in Plantation, Florida, and Gallery 47 as well as Bizarre Bazaar Ltd. in New York, all specializing in top perfume bottles. Here you can take a look at the pieces in a more intimate environment than an auctioneer's salesroom. Museums, too, are always worth a visit, the most prominent being the Musée des Arts Décoratifs in Paris and the Gulbenkian Museum in Lisbon, although many museums throughout the world have examples worth your visit.

The 1932 catalog published by Lalique et Cie is of course invaluable to anyone interested in his glass, and worth investing in as well are Nicholas M. Dawes's *Lalique Glass,* Patricia Bayer and Mark Waller's *The Art of René Lalique,* and the Lalique company's recently published *Lalique* by Marie-Claude Lalique. The most recent book on perfume bottles in general is *Commercial Perfume Bottles* by Jacquelyne Jones-North. Consult the bibliography for further titles. And be on the lookout for vintage magazines that may have advertisements or articles featuring Lalique flacons. Not only are these of historical interest, but they're often handsome enough to frame and display, preferably next to the bottle(s) they depict!

Look for the flacons that are in excellent condition and are "right," that is, with the correct stopper, no smoothed-down or cutoff areas, no diminished size due to ground-down bases or rims. For the uninitiated it's often hard to discern this, but the illustrations in this book should be of great assistance in this regard. A small, unnoticeable chip may be inconsequential, although generally it will lower a piece's value. Of course, bottles that were never opened and still contain their original scents are highly prized, as are those retaining vintage labels, tassels, *patine,* etc., or that are in the original box or package, which can add 50 to 100 percent to the value.

Some bottles are beset with so-called "glass disease," caused by chemicals in water, which clouds the clear bottle in an unsightly manner. There is no surefire way to remove this, so don't be disappointed if, when you get home from the shop or market, you can't scrub off all the scum. If a brownish stain—residue from old perfume —covers the inside of the bottle, try cleaning it with fingernail polish remover, denture cleanser, or denatured alcohol. Carefully wash all bottles, but especially those with *patine* or enameling. Plain warm water and soap are the best cleaners, but be cautious when you are washing a delicately molded stopper or a fairly thin-walled flacon. And if the bottle sports a label, pour soapy water only in the inside; use a cotton swab to carefully clean the exterior around the label.

Sometimes hard-to-remove stoppers can be unstuck by running warm water around the neck of the flacon and gently easing the stopper out, but other times it's best to leave a piece as is, lest the stopper break off (as has been known to hap-

pen). Since Lalique's stoppers were made and inserted according to the *bouchon à l'émeri* method, try gently twisting the stopper to get it out; but, again, don't force it.

When displaying bottles, avoid placing them in direct sunlight, and think about buying a lighted display cabinet, or vitrine, if your collection becomes big enough to warrant it. Make sure a steady temperature and atmosphere are maintained wherever you keep your flacons, since extremes may crack or even burst a bottle.

For transporting from auction/flea market to home, for instance, disposable diapers cushion bottles even better than bubble wrap or Styrofoam "peanuts." They're more or less the right size, plus they have tape already attached. Remember to remove the stopper and pack it separately—but don't lose it, and don't forget which bottle it came out of!

POSTSCRIPT

We hope that this book is interesting and informative for collectors both novice and experienced as well as for those interested in the art of René Lalique. From the sheer volume of flacons it's easy to see why Lalique is still considered the master perfume bottle designer/maker, a seminal and significant figure in the *haute couture de flaconnage* even today, more than four decades after his death. His talents as a goldsmith and all-around glass designer and producer have been well known for some time, but the extent of his flacon production—and indeed his influence vis-à-vis the art of the twentieth-century perfume bottle—had only been covered cursorily, in articles and sections within larger books. Let the words of Pierre Dinand, one of the greatest perfume bottle designers working today,[1] stand as the ultimate tribute from artist to artist. He said that René Lalique was, simply, *"le plus grand artiste joaillier pour flacons de parfum."*

APPENDIX

EXPLANATION

THIS BOOK IS BASED ON DATA COMPILED BY MARY Lou and Glenn Utt over the years, covering every known Lalique perfume bottle that could be confirmed. Confirmation was based on authenticity of signature, verification from at least two reliable sources, and/or personal examination of the bottle itself. Certainly errors have been made and new designs will be discovered later. Information sources included auction catalogs, private collections, museums, perfume companies, existing literature, Lalique and perfume bottle dealers, and, of course, Cristal Lalique.

Perfume, scent, cologne, and eau de toilette bottles are included. Atomizers, scent burners, *brûle parfums,* and other *garnitures de toilette* are not included.

The tables are arranged as follows and contain the information and codes as shown:

I. Pre-1945 Production (René Lalique)
    A. For perfume companies
        1. Manufacturer Known
        2. Manufacturer Unknown
    B. For sale in Lalique outlets (Maison Lalique)
        1. Those not in 1932 catalog
        2. Those in the 1932 catalog
    C. Experimental/unique designs

II. Post-1945 Production (Marc Lalique and Marie-Claude Lalique designs, with some carryover of prewar models)
    A. For perfume companies
    B. For sale in Lalique outlets (Cristal Lalique)

Perfume Companies. The designs are grouped, where known, by company.

Perfume/Bottle Name. The name given to the bottle or the name of the perfume for which it was generally used is given. In some cases, of course, a bottle was used for a number of different scents.

Figure. The figure number refers to illustrations.

Size. Dimensions given are for the height, except where otherwise noted. Dimensions are given in centimeters (2.5 cm equals 1 in.).

Signature. The signature type is coded per the table on page 131. Some bottles, of course, are not signed.

Rarity. The relative quantity of examples available has been graded from 1 (most rare) to 6 (most plentiful) on the basis of the authors' judgment.

Value. The relative value of the different designs has been ranked from A (most valuable) to E (least valuable) on the basis of the authors' judgment.

Code. The bottle code is based on an abbreviation for the name of the perfume company (*C* for Coty, *LL* for Lucien Lelong, *Gab* for Gabilla, etc.), using *ML* for Maison Lalique, *CL* for Cristal Lalique, and *UK* for unknown. Other than for the Maison Lalique models from the 1932 catalog (which retain their original 400s to 600s series), the bottles for each company are numbered consecutively (C-1 for the first Coty listing, etc.). Pre-1945 flacons begin with a single digit, whereas postwar models begin with 100.

The authors would greatly appreciate knowing of potential additions to the list, errors, and other new information. They can be addressed as follows:

Mr. & Mrs. Glenn Utt
P.O. Box 292
Palm Desert, CA 92261

A summary of the tabulations follows, which categorizes the 288 listings by company, period, and designer.

DESIGN SUMMARY AND TABLE INDEX*

Pre-1945**	Models	Pre-1945**	Models	Post-1945**	Models
Alpy (Al)	1	Lengyal (Len)	1	Lancôme (Lan)	4
Anna (An)	1	Lionçeau (Lio)	1	Marcel Rochas (Ro)	2
Arys (A)	14	Lournay (Lor)	1	Molinard (M)	4
Burmann (Bur)	1	Louvre (Lu)	2	Morabito (Mor)	1
Canarina (Can)	1	L. T. Piver (P)	1	Nina Ricci (NR)	16
Claire (Cl)	2	Lucien Lelong (LL)	2	Raphael (R)	1
Colgate (Col)	1	Magnum (Mag)	1	Worth (W)	7
Corday (Cor)	1	Maison Lalique (ML)			35
Coryse (Cse)	1	(1932 Catalog)	55		
Coty (C)	16	Maison Lalique (ML) (Others)	23	Cristal Lalique (CL)	
Delettrez (Del)	2	Martial et Armand (M&A)	1	(Current Models)	12
de Vigny (deV)	3	Molinard (M)	5	Cristal Lalique (CL)	
D'Heraud (D)	12	Molyneux (Mol)	1	(Discontinued Models)	7
D'Orsay (DO)	20	Oviatt (O)	1		
Erasmic (Era)	1	Rallet (Ra)	1	TOTAL	54
Fioret (Fio)	1	Raquel Meller (RM)	1	GRAND TOTAL	
Forvil (F)	13	Renaud/Lubin (Rel)	2	RECONCILIATION	
Fragonard (Fr)	1	Roger et Gallet (R&G)	10	Pre-1945	253
Gabilla (Gab)	4	Rosine (Ros)	1	Post-1945	54
Galeries Lafayette (GL)	1	Rotterdam Lloyd (RL)	1		307
Guerlain (G)	1	Saks Fifth Avenue (Saks)	1		
Houbigant (H)	6	Tokalon (To)	1	Deduct	
House of Gal (Gal)	1	Veolay (Veo)	1	Postwar	
Institut de Beauté (IB)	1	Volnay (Vo)	6	Carryovers†	-19
Isabey (Is)	1	Worth (W)	12	GRAND TOTAL	288
Jay Thorpe Co. (JT)	1	Unknown Parfumers	9		
Jean De Parys (JP)	3	TOTAL	253		
Lalo (Lal)	1				

* Does not include 11 experimental models herein cataloged.

** Companies are listed in order of appearance in the tables that follow. Fifty-five companies in all.

† Postwar model carryovers: Worth 5, Molinard 4, Cristal Lalique 10.

130

The vast majority of Lalique perfumes bear a signature, but a few do not. Generally, the signature "R. Lalique" signifies pre-1945 and "Lalique" means post-1945. However, some of the early bottles are without the "R." in the signature.

Courtesy Bonhams—London

R. I. AI.IQUE

Mark no. 1,
sand blasted or acid stamped onto the article

R. Lalique

Mark no. 2,
engraved mark (facsimile of René Lalique's signature)

R LALIQUE

Mark no. 3,
wheel-cut

R. Lalique

Mark no. 4,
etched mark with appearance of being scratched, similar to mark no. 2

R LALIQUE

Mark no. 5,
finely engraved mark

R. LALIQUE

Mark no. 6,
molded mark, in relief or intaglio

131

Mark no. 7,
intaglio

R.LALIQUE

Mark no. 8,
molded in relief

R LALIQUE

Mark no. 9,
molded in relief

R LALIQUE

Mark no. 10,
molded in relief

R Lalique France

Mark no. 11,
Similar in method to mark no. 4

Mark no. 12,
'Verrerie D' Alsace' VDA mark used for a short
period after the factory opened

LALIQUE

Mark no. 13,
Cristal Lalique mark, similar to mark no. 1

Mark no. 14,
molded "RL"

Mark no. 15,
Same as Mark no. 8, without "R"

Mark no. 16,
Same as Mark no. 2, without "R"

UK—Unknown   NS—Not Signed

Postwar signatures are all without the "R" and are
simply coded:
E = Engraved/Script   M = Molded
SB = Sand Blasted

132

TABLES

◆

Pre-1945 Production (René Lalique)
for Perfume Companies and Maison Lalique

ALPY (Al)

Al-1 Lavande Fig. 31

Size: 21 cm   Mark: 8   Rarity: 3   Value: C

Spreading branches with stain.

ANNA (An)

An-1 Globular base/tiered stopper Fig. 217

Size: 9 cm   Mark: 9   Rarity: 1   Value: B/C

1927. Stopper similar to Imprudence (W-7). Not known whether Anna is name of company or of perfume (possibly for Worth).

ARYS (A)

A-1 Feuilles Fig. 26

Size: 8.5 cm   Mark: 6   Rarity: 3   Value: C/D
   11   cm

1922. Perfume Faisons un Rêve also in this bottle. Pointed stopper.

A-2 Premier Oui Fig. 219

Size: 12   cm   Mark: 2/10   Rarity: 2   Value: C
   16   cm
   18.5 cm

1919. Chypre also in this bottle. Cylinder in three sizes.

A-3 Faisons un Rêve Fig. 120

Size: 10.5 cm to   Mark: 8   Rarity: 2   Value: B/C
   17   cm

Pre-1922. Ball stopper. Three sizes.

A-4 Le Lilas Fig. 121

Size: 10.5 cm   Mark: 8   Rarity: 2   Value: B/C
   14   cm

1920s. La Violette also in this bottle. Blue stain on stopper.

A-5 L'Amour dans le Coeur Fig. 120

Size: 10 cm   Mark: 8   Rarity: 4   Value: D
   15 cm

1919. Large size without cupid design in center.

A-6 Croyez Moi Fig. 120

Size: 8 cm   Mark: 8   Rarity: 4   Value: D
   9.5 cm

1919. Molded circles of leaves on a sphere. Two sizes.

A-7 Butterflies on bottle and stopper Fig. 125

Size: 15 cm   Mark: 8   Rarity: 1   Value: B/C

Brown stain. Also was made with butterflies on stopper only.

A-8 Tapering cylinder/pointed stopper Fig. 121

Size: 10   cm   Mark: 8   Rarity: 3/4   Value: C/D
   11.5 cm

Stylized design on base.

A-9 Un Jour Viendra Fig. 219

Size: 12.5 cm   Mark: 14   Rarity: 4   Value: D
   19   cm

1919. Border design on small version.

A-10 Tapered cylinder/conical stopper Fig. 122

Size: 14 cm   Mark: 14   Rarity: 1/2   Value: B/C
   22 cm

Collection Marie-Claude Lalique.

A-11 Pyramid with button stopper Fig. 175

Size: 8 cm   Mark: 14   Rarity: 1/2   Value: B

Stylized flower design.

A-12 Rien que du Bonheur Fig. 124

Size: 12 cm   Mark: 8   Rarity: 1/2   Value: B

Ball stopper.

A-13 Tapered cylinder to button stopper Fig. 123

Size: 18 cm   Mark: 7   Rarity: 1/2   Value: B/C

Similar to A-3. Collection Marie-Claude Lalique.

A-14 Rose Fig. 126

Size: 13   cm   Mark: 10   Rarity: 2   Value: B/C
   15.5 cm

Coiled rosebush thorns stopper, frosted and with stain, otherwise clear.

BURMANN (Bur)

Bur-1 La Sirène Fig. 204, 218

Size: 11 cm   Mark: 7   Rarity: 1   Value: A+

Also a larger size (19 cm) with a hole in stopper and slightly different mermaid pose in Collection Marie-Claude Lalique, probably experimental.

CANARINA (Can)

Can-1 Les Yeux Bléus Fig. 188

Size: 5 cm   Mark: 8   Rarity: 2/3   Value: B

1920s. Like multitude of eyes. Blue glass, white stain.

CLAIRE (Cl)

Cl-1 Orée Fig. 202

Size: 8 cm   Mark: 15   Rarity: 2   Value: B
   intaglio

133

Same as Louvre (Lu-1) except brand name on stopper and draped girl rather than nude on base. Signed on stopper.

Cl-2 Orée (Eau de Toilette) Fig. 203

Size: 17 cm   Mark: 7   Rarity: 1   Value: B/C

See Carafe Pyramidale no. 3152, plate 96, 1932 Lalique catalog. Daisies design on disk stopper. Base clear in carafe style. Collection Marie-Claude Lalique.

COLGATE (Col)

Col-1 Orchis Fig. 165

Size: 9 cm   Mark: 8   Rarity: 1   Value: C

Frosted bouquet design.

CORDAY (Cor)

Cor-1 Tzigane Fig. 129, 187

Size: 10 cm to   Mark: 10   Rarity: 4   Value: C/D
21 cm

Introduced 1938. Five sizes.

CORYSE (Cse)

Cse-1 Vinca Fig. 205

Size: 9 cm   Mark: 8   Rarity: 1   Value: A

1928. Two rows of overlapping black enamel squares on frosted square flask body in shape of X.

COTY (C)

C-1 L'Effleurt de Coty Fig. 21

Size: 11 cm   Mark: 15   Rarity: 1/2   Value: A/B

Probably the first Lalique bottle for Coty, circa 1908. Label molded in the glass. Brown stain. Two examples seen without "L'Effleurt de Coty" in the mold, possibly for Maison Lalique.

C-2 L'Entraînement (a.k.a. Le Baiser) Fig. 23

Size: 9 cm   Mark: 5   Rarity: 1   Value: A+

1911. Collection Marie-Claude Lalique and Musée des Arts Décoratifs, Paris. Stain. Male and female kissing one side and walking together on other side. Used for various perfumes.

C-3 Ambre Antique Fig. 22

Size: 15 cm   Mark: 8   Rarity: 3/4   Value: B/C

1910. One of the first for Coty. Stain usually brown.

C-4 Styx (a.k.a. Guêpes) Fig. 24

Size: 12 cm   Mark: 15   Rarity: 2   Value: B

1910–13. Similar to *Carnette Fleur* (Maison Lalique, n. 510). Stopper comes with stem separate or as one piece. Possibly a very early Maison Lalique presentation as well. Musée des Arts Décoratifs model is unsigned.

C-5 Au Coeur des Calices Fig. 25

Size: 7 cm   Mark: 15   Rarity: 1   Value: A+

1912. Blue glass. Bee stopper.

C-6 Série Epius (a.k.a. Lézards) Fig. 26

Size: 15.5 cm   Mark: 4   Rarity: 3   Value: D
19 cm
23 cm

1921. Used for perfumes Paris, Chypre, and Styx.

C-7 Masques Fig. 27

Size: 10 cm   Mark: NS   Rarity: 1   Value: B

1913. Six masks/faces on stopper. Stopper comes with stem separate or as one piece. Possibly a very early Maison Lalique presentation as well. Musée des Arts Décoratifs, Paris.

C-8 Cyclamen (A) (a.k.a. Libellule) Fig. 28

Size: 14 cm   Mark: 6   Rarity: 2   Value: A/B
and 15
intaglio

1913. Earliest version of *Cyclamen* with molded "Cyclamen, Coty-Paris" on stopper. Later version without "R." in signature.

C-9 Cyclamen (B) Fig. 29

Size: 13.5 cm   Mark: 15   Rarity: 2   Value: A/B
intaglio

1920s. Stopper plain. L'Aimant also in this bottle.

C-10 Cyclamen (C) Fig. 30

Size: 13.5 cm   Mark: 15   Rarity: 1   Value: A/B
intaglio

Same as *Cyclamen* (A) except different neck/stopper configurations. Sometimes signed "Lalique Dépose," as in example from Collection of Marie-Claude Lalique.

C-11 L'Origan Fig. 31

Size: 27 cm   Mark: NS   Rarity: 1   Value: A

1910s. Frosted rings of rose blossoms. Very tall eau de toilette.

C-12 Série Toilette (a.k.a. Briar) Fig. 18

Size: 11 cm   Mark: 7   Rarity: 4   Value: D/E
13.5 and
12 cm   others

This bottle with at least twelve different scents. Many unsigned examples probably made at Legras & Company prior to opening of Lalique facility. See Nicholas M. Dawes, *Lalique Glass* (New York: Crown Publishers, 1986).

C-13 Muguet Fig. 29

Size: 8 cm   Mark: 7   Rarity: 4/5   Value: D
10 cm

Also, other versions sold in sets with various labels, metal stopper, and unsigned. Baccarat produced essentially the same bottle (Fig. 307, *Baccarat/"The Perfume Bottles,"* [Paris: Addor & Associes, 1987]) and another (Fig. 754) with greater slope in the shoulder, all three with same stopper. Apparently it was not unusual for designers/perfumers/bottle makers to intermix from time to time.

C-14 Lipas Pourpre Fig. 32

Size: 6.5 cm   Mark: 7   Rarity: 4   Value: D

1914. Stopper with waves design. Identical bottle seen with Louvre (department store) label with Oeillet perfume (Lu-2). Many unsigned examples, probably made by different factory at later date.

C-15 Héliotrope Fig. 33

Size: 6.5 cm   Mark: NS   Rarity: 3   Value: C
8 cm

Collection Marie-Claude Lalique. Two stopper versions and two sizes.

C-16 Émeraude Fig. 34

Size: 9 cm   Mark: 10   Rarity: 1   Value: C

Flower decoration on frosted stopper. Clear oval flask base.

Note: Coty was René Lalique's first commercial client for perfume bottles. Pfizer International acquired Coty in 1963.

D E L E T T R E Z   (D e l)

Del-1 Inalda (A) Fig. 189, 190

Size: 9 cm   Mark: 9   Rarity: 1   Value: B

Introduced into the U.S. in 1934. Rings with black enamel dots.

Del-2 Inalda (B) Fig. 189

Size: 8 cm   Mark: UK   Rarity: 1   Value: B

Introduced into the U.S. in 1935. Bubbles and scallops square flask design. Seen only in advertisement.

D E   V I G N Y   (d e V)

deV-1 D'où Vient'Il? Fig. 198

Size: 9.5 cm   Mark: 8   Rarity: 1   Value: A

1922. Butterflies design.

deV-2 Jamerose Fig. 199

Size: 12 cm   Mark: 8   Rarity: 2   Value: C

Introduced in 1924. Clear pointed stopper.

deV-3 L'Ambre Fig. 197

Size: 15 cm   Mark: 8   Rarity: 1   Value: A

Same design as carafe *Marguerites Bouchon Pointe,* plate 97, number 3161. 1932 Lalique catalog. Collection Marie-Claude Lalique.

D ' H E R A U D   (D H)

DH-1 Les Feuillages Fig. 176

Size: 9 cm   Mark: 8   Rarity: 1   Value: A

Two-bird stopper—tiaralike.

DH-2 Phalène (A) Fig. 152

Size: 9 cm   Mark: 8   Rarity: 1   Value: A

Introduced into U.S. in 1923. Woman's figure with butterfly wings/arms. In orange glass and in frosted clear glass with black stain. Flower blossom stopper. Also known as *Amberina* in orange.

DH-3 Phalène (B) Fig. 153

Size: 9.5 cm   Mark: 8   Rarity: 1   Value: A

Same as above except upright flat, spherical stopper. Seen only in orange.

DH-4 Cologne d'Heraud Fig. 243

Size: 14.5 cm   Mark: 10   Rarity: 5   Value: C/D
17 cm
20.5 cm

At least three sizes. Molded and stained "D'Heraud" in center and "Cologne" on reverse.

DH-5 Chypre Fig. 155

Size: 8 cm   Mark: 2   Rarity: 2   Value: C
13 cm

Brown stain in indented columns.

DH-6 Violette Fig. 157

Size: 8 cm   Mark: 8   Rarity: 2   Value: C

Molded "D'Heraud" in center and "Violette" on reverse.

DH-7 Origan Fig. 156

Size: 14 cm   Mark: 2   Rarity: 2   Value: B/C

Molded "Origan" design in center with brown stain.

DH-8 Flask—rectangular Fig. 154

Size: 12.5 cm   Mark: 2   Rarity: 2   Value: B/C

Molded on sides with "D'Heraud" and "Paris." On front "Lotion," on back "OR——" (probably "Origan"). Brown stain. Greek-key-motif stopper.

DH-9 Semis des Fleurs (A) Fig. 158

Size: 7 cm   Mark: 8   Rarity: 1   Value: A/B

1923. Sphere with indented flower heads. Stopper similar to *Phalène* (A) (DH-2).

DH-10 Semis des Fleurs (B) Fig. 165

Size: 9 cm   Mark: 15   Rarity: 1   Value: B

Indented flower heads on cylinder. Flower design almost the same as DH-9. Stopper similar, but slightly different.

DH-11 Marjolaine Fig. 159

Size: 11 cm   Mark: NS   Rarity: 1/2   Value: B/C

Woman's face in center of square flask.

DH-12 Rose

Size: 8 cm   Mark: 8   Rarity: 1   Value: B/C

Square flask with frosted, brown stained roundels. One side decorated with a rose, reverse with leafage.

D ' O R S A Y   (D O)

DO-1 Ambre D'Orsay Figs. 101, 103, 102

Size: 13 cm   Mark: 15   Rarity: 3 Black   Value: B/C
1 Clear   A/B
1 Clear   A
with eagles

1913. Black and clear glass. Sometimes seen without "Ambre D'Orsay" molding—may be Maison Lalique and/or sold only in France and the clear version with eagles design on stopper is signed intaglio, upside down, and was made for Maison Lalique. (ML-3).

DO-2 Mystère (a.k.a. Lézards) Figs. 101, 104

Size: 9.5 cm   Mark: 8   Rarity: 3 Black   Value: B/C
1 Clear   A/B

1915. Black and clear glass. Clear version (Musée des Arts Décoratifs, Paris) has script signature and was possibly *Lézards* for Maison Lalique.

DO-3 Statue of girl on frosted sphere Fig. 105

Size: 10 cm   Mark: 7   Rarity: 2/3   Value: B

Maison Lalique (ML-18) is another version with clear base.

DO-4 Grâce D'Orsay Fig. 109

Size: 13 cm   Mark: 9   Rarity: 1   Value: A +

1915–20. Stain brown.

DO-5 L'Elégance Fig. 107

Size: 9.5 cm   Mark: 8   Rarity: 1/2   Value: B

Two robed dancing girls. Also used with Ambre perfume. Brown stain.

DO-6 Le Succès Fig. 106

Size: 9.5 cm   Mark: 8   Rarity: 1   Value: A

Commercial version of *Amphytrite.* (ML-514).

DO-7 Poésie D'Orsay Fig. 98

Size: 14 cm   Mark: 10   Rarity: 1   Value: A/B

1914. Stained blue or brown.

DO-8 Série Roses Fig. 113

Size: 8 cm   Mark: 8   Rarity: 4   Value: D
      9.5 cm

Often sold in set of three in leather case. Seven different perfumes found in this bottle. The "standard" D'Orsay flask by Lalique.

DO-9 Leurs Âmes Fig. 108

Size: 13 cm   Mark: 7   Rarity: 1/2   Value: A +
              NS   1 plastic   B/C

1913. Comes with and without molded "Leurs Ames." Without molded "Leurs Ames"—possibly Maison Lalique. Also, special 25th U.S. anniversary presentation with plastic tiara for perfume Belle de Jour—at $1 in 1940.

DO-10 Chypre Fig. 111

Size: 6.5 cm   Mark: 14   Rarity: 3   Value: C
      8.5 cm

Stylized flower design on sphere.

DO-11 Le Lys Fig. 110

Size: 10 cm   Mark: 10   Rarity: 5   Value: C/D
      to
      21.5 cm

Various stains. Flower design. Four sizes. "Le Lys D'Orsay' molded on stopper.

DO-12 Rose Ambrée Fig. 115

Size: 7.5 cm   Mark: 8   Rarity: 2/3   Value: C

Five beaded columns each side.

DO-13 Roses D'Orsay Fig. 99

Size: 14 cm   Mark: 14   Rarity: 2   Value: B

Advertised 1920. Cylinder with metal band of Grecian figures. Crystal by Baccarat, metal work by Lalique. Signature stamped in metal. Also Fleurettes version and used for scent Ambre D'Orsay.

DO-14 Dandy Fig. 100

Size: 10.5 cm   Mark: 8   Rarity: 1 set   Value: A +
      box
      6 cm bottle   1/2 bottle   B

Black glass box of four bow-tie-shaped perfumes and one powder box. D'Orsay crest on box cover. Used for various perfumes. 100 sets were originally made in black. 1927.

DO-15 Illusion Fig. 114

Size: 6 cm   Mark: 8 neck   Rarity: 3   Value: C
      9 cm
      11.5 cm

Clear square "box" shape with beaded edges. Frosted cover with floral design over inside stopper. Three sizes. Small size with roses, others cornflowers.

DO-16 Square flask/double dot borders Fig. 116

Size: 8 cm   Mark: 8   Rarity: 2   Value: C/D

Rectangular stopper same as for DO-12 and DO-17.

DO-17 Square flask/single dot borders Fig. 117

Size: 8 cm   Mark: 8   Rarity: 3   Value: D

Base same as DO-8. Stopper same as DO-12 and DO-16.

DO-18 Gavotte Bleue Fig. 118

Size: 8.5 cm   Mark: 8   Rarity: 1   Value: B/C
      10 cm

Also with perfume Leur Coeur D'Orsay and others. Blue button stopper with holes for silk cord. Also an eau de toilette size made by Baccarat.

DO-19 Chypre (Eau de Toilette) Fig. 119

Size: 24 cm   Mark: 4   Rarity: 1   Value: A

Tall oval with borders of blue enameled flower heads.

DO-20 Eucalyptus Fig. 83

Size: 4.5 cm   Mark: 15   Rarity: 1   Value: A

Pendant with silk cord. Identical to ML-7 except molded D'Orsay on one side.

Note: D'Orsay was Lalique's third commercial client for perfume bottles.

E R A S M I C   (E r a)

Era-1 Circular flask Fig. 200

Size: 8.5 cm   Mark: 10   Rarity: 1   Value: A

Stopper molded "Erasmic." Lady in center of two butterflies.

F I O R E T   (F i o)

Fio-1 Chose Promise Fig. 193

Size: 13 cm   Mark: 8   Rarity: 1   Value: A/B

Stopper with nude design.

F O R V I L   (F)

F-1 Le Parfum NN Fig. 101

Size: 9.5 cm   Mark: 8   Rarity: 1   Value: A

Black glass. Molded letters and white wash.

F-2 Le Parfum Noir Fig. 136

Size: 9.5 cm   Mark: 8   Rarity: 1   Value: A

Same as *NN* except molding of different name. One known without molded perfume and Forvil names.

F-3 Le Corail Rouge Fig. 139

Size: 10 cm   Mark: 8   Rarity: 1   Value: A +

Red enamel

F-4 La Perle Noire Fig. 137

Size: 11.5 cm   Mark: 8   Rarity: 2   Value: A/B

1922. Simulated glass pearl in center.

F-5 Les 5 Fleurs (A) (a.k.a. Daisies) Fig. 147

Size: 8 cm   Mark: 10   Rarity: 5   Value: C/D
      10 cm

Often sold in box of three in leather/felt case.

F-6 Les 5 Fleurs (B) (a.k.a. Celtic) Fig. 145

Size: 6.5 cm to   Mark: 8   Rarity: 5   Value: C/D
      19.5 cm

Advertised 1926. Usually as eau de toilette. Black enamel. Three sizes.

F-7 Chypre (a.k.a. Wysteria) Fig. 148

Size: 7.5 cm   Mark: 10   Rarity: 5   Value: C/D
      9 cm

Box of three often seen with six different perfumes. Small size seen with brass case.

F-8 Relief (a.k.a. Coquilles) Fig. 149

Size: 9 cm to 21 cm   Mark: 8   Rarity: 4   Value: C/D

Usually for eau de cologne. Four sizes. Also with Les 5 Fleurs.

F-9 Trois Valses (a.k.a. Frise d'Enfants) Fig. 146

Size: 10 cm   Mark: 8   Rarity: 2   Value: B

Gold stain on center cupid design.

F-10 Narcisse (a.k.a. Anémones) Fig. 146

Size: 6 cm   Mark: 8   Rarity: 1   Value: A/B

Sphere with four deeply indented flower heads. Also with perfume Les Yeux Noirs.

F-11 Les Anémones Fig. 143

Size: 9.5 cm   Mark: 9   Rarity: 2   Value: B/C

1925. Design like vase number 1179, 1932 catalog. Also see current Cristal Lalique vase number 11613 *(Deux Anémones)*. Enamel in flower centers.

F-12 1925 Flacon Fig. 150

Size: 12.5 cm   Mark: 9   Rarity: 1   Value: A

Cylinder with beaded design like columns at entrance to 1925 Paris Exposition. Black enamel decoration.

F-13 "5" Fig. 151

Size: 7 cm   Mark: 8   Rarity: 1   Value: B

Triangular frosted designs coming in from the four sides of the rectangular flask.

Note to F-5: Design appears to be same as Emiliane powder box 49 BIS, number 90, 1932 catalog. Le Lys perfume for D'Orsay and D'Orsay powder box with D'Orsay name on top also same basic design.

Note to F-9, 10 and 11: All bottles were available in Forvil specialties Les 5 Fleurs, Hymenée, Trois Valses, Les Yeux Doux, À Vos Ordres, Anémones, Chypre, and Lavande.

FRAGONARD (Fr)

Fr-1 Larger version of Rosine bottle Fig. 127

Size: 14 cm   Mark: 9   Rarity: 1/2   Value: C

Not clear how or why Fragonard, Roger et Gallet, and Rosine bottles are of same design, but slightly different stoppers. All are clearly molded "R. Lalique."

GABILLA (Gab)

Gab-1 La Violette Fig. 175

Size: 9 cm   Mark: 10   Rarity: 2   Value: A/B

1925. Violettes design—enameled blue.

Gab-2 Toutes les Fleurs Fig. 176

Size: 10 cm   Mark: 8   Rarity: 1/2   Value: B

Small flower design. "Cross" base.

Gab-3 Lilas (a.k.a. Millefleur) Fig. 80

Size: 9 cm   Mark: 10   Rarity: 2   Value: B

1926. Pod shape with *millefleur* (1000 Flowers) design.

Gab-4 Glycine Fig. 177

Size: 11 cm   Mark: 10   Rarity: 1/2   Value: B

Tapered cylinder, floral design with blue stain. Rope-knot stopper.

GALERIES LAFAYETTE (GL)

GL-1 La Feuillaison Fig. 24

Size: 8 cm   Mark: 7   Rarity: 1   Value: B/C

Same bottle as Coty (C-13—*Muguet*); different stopper.

Note: Claire, Louvre, and Galeries Lafayette bottles/perfumes appear to be Coty promotional perfume brands in Lalique bottles for various department stores. Wanamaker in Philadelphia, Bloomingdale's in New York, Harrods in London, Louvre and Galeries Lafayette in Paris, and others (1925–27). Another bottle (unknown, but probably Lalique) was previously done for Harrods in 1914 for the Coty perfume Meteor; label known to be designed by Lalique. A Styx label (Coty) for the Paris department store Le Printemps is also on file at Cristal Lalique.

GUERLAIN (G)

G-1 Bouquet de Faunes (a.k.a. Guernais) Fig. 178

Size: 10 cm 11 cm 13.5 cm   Mark: NS   Rarity: 4   Value: C

1925. Lalique designed, but not known to be signed.

HOUBIGANT (H)

H-1 La Belle Saison Fig. 166

Size: 10 cm 12.5 cm   Mark: 8   Rarity: 2/3   Value: B

Introduced into the U.S. in 1926. Brown stain. Two sizes.

H-2 Le Temps de Lilas Fig. 165

Size: 8.5 cm 11 cm   Mark: 15   Rarity: 4   Value: C

U.S. advertisements in 1922. Two sizes.

H-3 Ensemble Houbigant Fig. 169

Size: 14 cm box 5.5 cm bottles   Mark: 8   Rarity: 1/2 set   Value: A/B

Many different Houbigant perfumes in same bottles. Opalescent box cover with satin inner cover..

H-4 Triangle Flacon Fig. 168

Size: 5.5 cm   Mark: 8   Rarity: 2/3   Value: D/E

As in above ensemble.

H-5 Triangle Variations Fig. 168

Size: 5.5 cm   Mark: 15   Rarity: 1   Value: C

Three other stoppers. Two other designs on bottle. Collection Marie-Claude Lalique.

H-6 Chypre (a.k.a. Trellis) Fig. 167

Size: 8 cm   Mark: 6   Rarity: 4   Value: C/D

U.S. patent 1922. Various stains.

HOUSE OF GAL (Gal)

Gal-1 Gal-Madrid Fig. 209

Size: 4.5 cm   Mark: 9   Rarity: 1   Value: A/B

1925. Leaf design. Stain. Spanish perfume company.

INSTITUT DE BEAUTÉ (IB)

IB-1 Klytia Fig. 208

Size: 9.5 cm   Mark: 2   Rarity: 1   Value: A

Institut de Beauté (Beauty Salon) was located on upper floors of shop next door to Lalique's at 26 Place Vendôme. Waves design.

ISABEY (Is)

Is-1 À Travers la Voilette Fig. 224

Size: 7.5 cm   Mark: 8   Rarity: 1   Value: B

Decorated with flower/leaf design in black and gold enamel by "Alix."

JAY-THORPE CO. (JT)

JT-1 Méchant mais Charmant Fig. 210

Size: 7 cm   Mark: 8   Rarity: 4   Value: C/D

Introduced in 1927. Frosted and with stain. Tulips design. "Jaytho" molded on front. Jay-Thorpe was a New York fashion salon.

Note: Also two larger bottles (10 and 12.5 cms) and a box of almost same design (with clear band in middle) usually without Lalique signature. The latter probably made by American source. Made with and without "Jaytho" in mold.

JEAN DE PARYS (JP)

JP-1 Chypre Fig. 182, 183

Size: 11.5 cm   Mark: 15   Rarity: 1   Value: A+

1925. Gold enamel with tassel. Two known complete with box and tassel.

JP-2 Sous le Gui Fig. 181, 183

Size: 10.5 cm   Mark: NS   Rarity: 1   Value: A+

1926. Black and gold with tassel. Three known complete with tassel. One seen in clear glass.

JP-3 Premier Désir Fig. 184

Size: 7.5 cm   Mark: 8   Rarity: 1   Value: A+

Flattened sphere of boxlike shape. Flower-decorated top/stopper with deep blue stain. Base clear with blue stained stripes. Molded on front of bottle "Premier Désir—Jean de Parys." Collection Marie-Claude Lalique.

Note: Bottles JP-1 and JP-2 were offered separately or in one leather presentation box. One known complete dual presentation set.

LALO (Lal)

Lal-1 Auteuil Fig. 195

Size: 4.5 cm   Mark: 8   Rarity: 1   Value: A+

One known, complete with original box.

LENGYAL (Len)

Len-1 Imperial Fig. 176

Size: 9 cm   Mark: 9   Rarity: 2   Value: B

Introduced 1936. Russian double-eagle design.

LIONCEAU (Lio)

Lio-1 Pierre Précieuse (a.k.a. Diamont) Fig. 191

Size: 9.5 cm   Mark: 5   Rarity: 1   Value: A+

1924. Gold enamel with glass "diamond" in center. Available with choice of thirteen different perfumes, including Parfum pour Blondes and Parfum pour Brunes.

LOURNAY (Lor)

Lor-1 L'Île d'Amour (Vanity Set) Fig. 222

Size: Box   Mark: UK   Rarity: 1   Value: A+
37.5 cm
by
50 cm

Advertisement of 1921 states: "Bottles of hand wrought glass, encrusted with copper, the work of Lalique, famous artist of France. No second set will be made from this design. The case 20″ x 15″ is of suede. PRICE $500."

LOUVRE (Lu)

Lu-1 Danaé Fig. 202

Size: 8 cm   Mark: 15   Rarity: 2   Value: B
intaglio

Brown stain. Figure of nude girl on base panel. Signature on stopper.

Lu-2 Oeillet Fig. 32

Size: 6.5 cm   Mark: 7   Rarity: 3   Value: C/D

Also see Coty (C-14). Same bottle with different label.

L. T. PIVER (P)

P-1 Misti (a.k.a. Papillons or Butterflies) Fig. 179

Size: 5 cm   Mark: 9   Rarity: 3   Value: C

Introduced into the U.S. in 1923. With butterfly design. Various stains. Later examples (1930s) with weak to no signature, appears to be due to age of mold. Uneven base with signature molded on edge. Also, a later version with stylized design, not Lalique.

Note: Piver is now part of Rhône-Poulenc (France).

LUCIEN LELONG (LL)

LL-1 Parfum A (a.k.a. Skyscraper) Fig. 129

Size: 10 cm   Mark: 10   Rarity: 2   Value: A
incl. case

1931. Metal case. Black or brown enamel. Perfumes A, B, C, N, and J.

LL-2 Étoile de Mer Fig. 219

Size: 7 cm   Mark: 9   Rarity: 1   Value: B/C
12 cm

U.S. patent filed November 16, 1931. Octagonal fluted cylinder. A similar non-Lalique version for

Lelong's Gardenia perfume also has been seen. It is clear with more shallow indentations.

Note: Lucien Lelong was absorbed by Coty in the 1950s.

M A G N U M (M a g)

Mag-1 Various Fig. 215

Size: 8 cm   Mark: 8   Rarity: 2/3   Value: C
and NS

Purse size. Magnum was a New York importer which repackaged perfumes, including various Coty, Dedon, and Caron perfumes—Narcisse Noir, Ambre Antique, Kiki, etc.

M A I S O N   L A L I Q U E   I N   1 9 3 2   C A T A L O G

ML-475 Cigales ★ (1910) ★★ Fig. 22, 37

Plate: 51   Size: 13 cm   Rarity: 2   Value: A/B

ML-476 Pavot Fig. 35

Plate: 52   Size: 7 cm   Rarity: 1   Value: A+

ML-477 Bouchon Papillon Fig. 53, 82

Plate: 53   Size: 6 cm   Rarity: 2   Value: A/B

ML-478 Petites Feuilles (1914) ★★ Fig. 38, 62

Plate: 51   Size: 10 cm   Rarity: 2   Value: B/C

ML-482 Lunaria (1914) ★★ Fig. 53

Plate: 53   Size: 8 cm   Rarity: 1/2   Value: A+

ML-483 Olives Fig. 38

Plate: 51   Size: 11 cm   Rarity: 3   Value: C

ML-484 Capricorne (1914) ★★ Fig. 42

Plate: 52   Size: 8 cm   Rarity: 2   Value: B/C

ML-485 Lentilles Fig. 37

Plate: 51   Size: 5 cm   Rarity: 3   Value: B/C

ML-486 Fleurs Concaves Fig. 53

Plate: 53   Size: 12 cm   Rarity: 2   Value: B/C

Also see CL-101.

ML-487 Panier de Roses Fig. 57

Plate: 52   Size: 10 cm   Rarity: 2   Value: B

ML-488 Rosace Figurines Fig. 55, 56

Plate: 53   Size: 11 cm   Rarity: 1   Value: A

Two known with gold enamel. Also see CL-110.

ML-489 Fougères (1913) (a.k.a. Bustes de Femme) Fig. 55

Plate: 53   Size: 9 cm   Rarity: 1   Value: A+

ML-490 Méplat, 2 Figurines (a.k.a. Bouchon Figurines) Fig. 51

Plate: 53   Size: 12 cm   Rarity: 1/2   Value: A+

ML-491 Salamandres ★ Fig. 36

Plate: 52   Size: 9.5 cm   Rarity: 2   Value: B

Also see CL-102.

ML-492 Nénuphar Fig. 52

Plate: 53   Size: 12 cm   Rarity: 1   Value: A

ML-493 Bouchon Fleurs de Pommier Fig. 46

Plate: 51   Size: 14 cm   Rarity: 1   Value: A+

ML-494 Bouchon Cassis ★ Fig. 43-45, 54

Plate: 51   Size: 11 cm   Rarity: 1/2   Value: A+

1912–1913.

ML-495 Bouchon Mûres ★ Fig. 54, 74

Plate: 51   Size: 11 cm   Rarity: 1   Value: A+

ML-496 Bouchon Hirondelles Fig. 48

Plate: 53   Size: 12 cm   Rarity: 1   Value: A+

Also a larger version with rounded tiara.

ML-497 Spirales Fig. 36

Plate: 52   Size: 10 cm   Rarity: 2   Value: B/C

ML-498 3 Guêpes Fig. 35

Plate: 52   Size: 12 cm   Rarity: 1   Value: A

ML-499 Anses et Bouchon Marguerite Fig. 35

Plate: 52   Size: 12 cm   Rarity: 1   Value: A/B

ML-500 Collerette avec Glands de Soie Fig. 66

Plate: 51   Size: 13 cm   Rarity: 1   Value: A/B

ML-501 Gros Fruits Fig. 54

Plate: 51   Size: 13 cm   Rarity: 1   Value: A

Also see Vo-1.

ML-502 Serpent Fig. 38, 40

Plate: 51   Size: 9 cm   Rarity: 2   Value: A/B

ML-503 Carré Hirondelles Fig. 35

Plate: 52   Size: 9 cm   Rarity: 4   Value: C

1914.

ML-504 Pan Fig. 52

Plate: 53   Size: 13 cm   Rarity: 3   Value: B/C

ML-505 4 Soleils Fig. 53, 67

Plate: 53   Size: 7.5 cm   Rarity: 1   Value: A+

ML-506 Lepage Fig. 36

Plate: 52   Size: 11.5 cm   Rarity: 1   Value: B

ML-507 Bouchon Eucalyptus ★ Fig. 47

Plate: 52   Size: 13.5 cm   Rarity: 1   Value: A+

ML-508 Telline ★ Fig. 42

Plate: 51   Size: 10 cm   Rarity: 3   Value: B

ML-510 Carnette Fleur Fig. 53

Plate: 53   Size: 12 cm   Rarity: 1/2   Value: A/B

ML-511 Plat, 3 Groupes 2 Danseuses Fig. 47, 49

Plate: 52   Size: 6 cm   Rarity: 1   Value: A+

ML-512 Plat, 6 Danseuses Fig. 47

Plate: 52   Size: 6 cm   Rarity: 1   Value: A+

ML-513 Glycines Fig. 52

Plate: 53   Size: 12 cm   Rarity: 3   Value: C

ML-514 Amphytrite★ Fig. 38, 40

Plate: 51   Size: 9.5 cm   Rarity: 2/3   Value: B

1922. Also see DO-6.

ML-515 Marquita★ Fig. 36, 41

Plate: 52   Size: 8.5 cm   Rarity: 3   Value: C

ML-516 Camille★ Fig. 37

Plate: 51   Size: 6 cm   Rarity: 3   Value: B/C

ML-517 Clamart★ Fig. 36

Plate: 52   Size: 11 cm   Rarity: 2   Value: B/C

1927.

ML-518 Palerme Fig. 37

Plate: 51   Size: 12 cm   Rarity: 3   Value: C/D

ML-519 Cactus★ Fig. 55, 245

Plate: 53   Size: 10 cm   Rarity: 4   Value: C/D

Also see RL-1 and CL-103.

ML-520 Amélie★ Fig. 52

Plate: 53   Size: 7.5 cm   Rarity: 3   Value: C

1927.

ML-521 Grégoire★ Fig. 37

Plate: 51   Size: 10 cm   Rarity: 2   Value: B/C

ML-522 Hélène (a.k.a. Lotus)★ Fig. 35

Plate: 52   Size: 7 cm   Rarity: 3   Value: C

ML-523 Ambroise★ Fig. 52, 96

Plate: 53   Size: 7.5 cm   Rarity: 3   Value: C

ML-524 Tantôt★ Fig. 38, 62

Plate: 51   Size: 15 cm   Rarity: 2   Value: B/C

ML-525 Muguet Fig. 64

Plate: 102   Size: 10 cm   Rarity: 1   Value: A/B

Also with pastel stoppers.

ML-526 Clairefontaine Fig. 65

Plate: 102   Size: 12 cm   Rarity: 2   Value: B

Also see CL-104.

ML-575-77 Fleurettes†‡ Fig. 26

Plate: 56   Size: 13 cm   Rarity: 5   Value: C/D
                    16 cm
                    20 cm

ML-590-93 Épines‡ Fig. 63

Plate: 55   Size: 8.5 cm   Rarity: 5   Value: C/D
                    to
                    12 cm

Also see Vo-2 and Vo-4.

ML-600-602 Perles‡ Fig. 26

Plate: 54   Size: 13.5 cm   Rarity: 4   Value: C/D
                    16.5 cm
                    20.5 cm

ML-609 Enfants‡ Fig. 246

Plate: 102   Size: 10 cm   Rarity: 3   Value: C

Also see CL-107.

ML-611, ML-612, ML-613 Myosotis‡ (a.k.a. Bouchon Figurine) Fig. 39

Plate: 57   Size: 23 cm   Rarity: 1   Value: A
        57   26 cm   2   A
        57   29 cm   2   A

Three different stoppers.

ML-615-18 Dahlia‡ Fig. 247

Plate: 115   Size: 9 cm   Rarity: 5   Value: C/D
                    to
                    21 cm

Also see CL-105.

ML-623-26 Duncan‡ Fig. 50

Plate: 114   Size: 19 cm   Rarity: 3   Value: C

In four widths, with one, two, three, or four nude figurines. Redesigned by Marc Lalique in 1974 with rectangular frosted stopper. See CL-106.

Note: ★ Available in color. Color versions can increase the value 50% to 100% +, depending on the model and color. ★★ ( ) Acquisition dates, Musée des Arts Décoratifs, the Louvre, Paris. † Available clear or frosted. ‡ Available with or without enamel.

ML-1 Deux Marguerites (a.k.a. Deux Fleurs) Fig. 79

Size: 8.5 cm   Mark: 2   Rarity: 4   Value: C/D

Double flower blossoms. Also postwar (CL-108).

ML-2 Hélène Fig. 248

Size: 14 cm   Mark: 2   Rarity: 3   Value: C
        22.5 cm

Also postwar (CL-109). Large version made with two rows of four panels. Grecian maiden figures.

ML-3 4 Figurines Fig. 102, 103

Size: 13 cm   Mark: 5   Rarity: 1   Value: A

Same as *Ambre D'Orsay* (DO-1) except clear, eagles design on stopper and intaglio signed (upside down). Quite likely DO-1 was adapted for D'Orsay from this Maison Lalique presentation, as others for D'Orsay and Coty may have been.

ML-4 2 Sirènes Fig. 82

Size: 5 cm   Mark: 15   Rarity: 1   Value: A

Purse-size flacon with two nude nymphs amid branches on each side.

ML-5 Satyr Fig. 74

Size: 9.25 cm   Mark: 1   Rarity: 1   Value: A

Devil's-head stopper with horns protruding out as stems.

ML-6 Jeunesse (a.k.a. Cherub) Fig. 80

Size: 10.5 cm   Mark: 1   Rarity: 1   Value: A

Nude cherub inside cylinder as extension of stopper.

ML-7 Eucalyptus Fig. 83

Size: 4.5 cm   Mark: 15   Rarity: 1/2   Value: A/B

Pendant of branches design with holes for silk cord. Also see DO-20, same but with "D'Orsay" in mold.

ML-8 L'Églantine de la Reine Fig. 76

Size: 10.5 cm   Mark: 15   Rarity: 1   Value: A +

Flower blossom tiara.

140

ML-9 Large reticulated stopper Fig. 61

Size: 12 cm   Mark: 15   Rarity: 1   Value: A+

Also signed "R. Lalique" in mold on stopper. A cachet version of the stopper was also made as Femme et Epines.

ML-10 Cylinder with dome Fig. 176

Size: 10 cm   Mark: 14   Rarity: 1   Value: A/B

Wisteria decoration and stained brown.

ML-11 Laurence Fig. 85

Size: 4 cm   Mark: 2   Rarity: 1   Value: A/B

1930. Perfume pendant. Shaped like an arrowhead with masks of four maidens. Three known.

ML-12 Oreilles Lezards Fig. 60

Size: 10.5 cm   Mark: 2   Rarity: 1   Value: A+

Stained wings of lizards. Two known.

ML-13 Oval flask with enameled leaves Fig. 59

Size: 8.5 cm   Mark: 8   Rarity: 1   Value: A

Black enamel. Two known.

ML-14 Tiara of blossoms and frosted base Fig. 77

Size: 15 cm   Mark: 2   Rarity: 1   Value: A+

One known.

ML-15 Tiara of blossoms and clear base Fig. 78

Size: 17.5 cm   Mark: 2   Rarity: 1   Value: A+

One known.

ML-16 Sirène Fig. 86, 87

Size: 12.5 cm   Mark: 8   Rarity: 1   Value: A

Correct stopper as shown in L'Art Décoratif Français, edited by Albert Lévy, *1918–25 Revue*. One known.

ML-17 Ovoid flask with concave center Fig. 88

Size: 7 cm   Mark: NS   Rarity: 1   Value: A

Flower or sunburst design with stylized disk stopper. Collection Marie-Claude Lalique. Also see Phillips sale, June 11, 1980, Lot 74.

ML-18 Statue of girl on clear sphere Fig. 68

Size: 10 cm   Mark: 7   Rarity: 1   Value: A+

Clear base except for "molten" raised and frosted free-form portion below neck. D'Orsay version (DO-3) has frosted/striped base. Collection Marie-Claude Lalique.

ML-19 Bullet-shaped cylindrical pendant Fig. 84

Size: 5 cm   Mark: 16   Rarity: 1   Value: A

Floral design, holes for silk cord and tassel. Seen in fitted case with CXC logo. Green and blue versions.

ML-20 Satyr/Masque Fig. 75

Size: 13.5 cm   Mark: 8   Rarity: 1   Value: A+

Oval flask. Frosted satyr with long horns. "Donut" stopper. Collection Marie-Claude Lalique.

ML-21 Ovoid flask with blossoms Fig. 69

Size: 9 cm   Mark: NS   Rarity: 1   Value: A
11 cm

Flower blossom design in center of bottle. Stained. See *Lalique par Lalique,* EDIPOP, Lausanne, 1977, p. 156. Collection Marie-Claude Lalique.

ML-22 Tapering flask Fig. 58

Size: 14 cm   Mark: NS   Rarity: 1   Value: A+

Minute flower heads down sides and on pointed stopper. Collection Marie-Claude Lalique.

ML-23 Hexagonal base/free-form stopper Fig. 70

Size: 15 cm   Mark: 15   Rarity: 1   Value: A+

Black enamel on the six edges of base. Stopper frosted. Possibly commercial. Collection Marie-Claude Lalique.

M A R T I A L   &   A R M A N D   (M & A)

M&A-1 Martial & Armand (a.k.a. Un Rien) Fig. 220

Size: 5 cm to   Mark: 8   Rarity: 1/2   Value: B
14 cm

1926. Coiffed females, Louis XV style. Stain. Perfumes Place Vendôme, Chypre, Ambre, and Un Rien. Five sizes, including two bottles of slightly different shape.

M O L I N A R D   (M)

M-1 Le Baiser du Faune (a.k.a. Embrasse and Légende) Fig. 160

Size: 14 cm   Mark: 8   Rarity: 2   Value: A/B
                intaglio

1930. Shown in the 1949 Centennial Molinard publication (1849–1949). Made with "R. Lalique" signature until early 1950s.

M-2 Calendal (a.k.a. Bacchantes and Habanita) Fig. 161

Size: 11.5 cm   Mark: 1 and 8   Rarity: 3   Value: B/C

1929. Various colors. Postwar (M-101). Made until early 1950s. Molded "R. Lalique" on lower face of bottle (faded in later years). Prewar with "R. Lalique" sandblasted on bottom; postwar sandblasted or stenciled "Lalique." Five known in 24K gold.

M-3 Madrigal (a.k.a. Amphore) Fig. 162

Size: 15 cm   Mark: 2   Rarity: 2   Value: B/C

Created 1930. Made until early 1950s. Prewar signed "R. Lalique," postwar "Lalique."

M-4 Les Îles d'Or Fig. 163

Size: 11 cm   Mark: 2   Rarity: 1/2   Value: B

1929. Made until early 1950s. Signed "R. Lalique" prewar, "Lalique" postwar (script). Same as current *Molinard de Molinard* (M-104) except for signature and clarity of mold.

M-5 Cariatides Fig. 164

Size: 11 cm   Mark: 8   Rarity: 1   Value: A

1928. Earliest Lalique bottle for Molinard. Discontinued approximately 1940. Six-faceted flask with floral border design and columns of caryatids.

M O L Y N E U X   (M o l)

Mol-1 Double square Fig. 221

Size: 8 cm   Mark: 8   Rarity: 1   Value: A/B
11.5 cm

1926. Base with interlocking squares design. Stopper in two versions: interlocking squares design and "M" figure. Collection Marie-Claude Lalique.

141

O V I A T T (O)

O-1 Le Parfum des Anges Fig. 211

Size: 8.5 cm   Mark: 10   Rarity: 3   Value: C

For opening of Oviatt Building, Los Angeles, 1927. Lalique also designed much of the decorative/architectural pieces and panels. The building is on the Historical Register (U.S.). Design includes the seal of the City of Los Angeles. Also with a tubular stopper, a metal cylinder stopper and without name of perfume in mold. Clear or charcoal gray.

R A L L E T (R a)

Ra-1 Soir Antique Fig. 192

Size: 7.5 cm   Mark: 8   Rarity: 1   Value: A/B

Square flask. Frosted design of nude and satyr. Coty bought Rallet in 1930.

R A Q U E L M E L L E R (R M)

RM-1 Rectangular flask Fig. 225

Size: 7.5 cm   Mark: 6   Rarity: 1   Value: A +

Enamel decoration of orange flower blossoms on black background. Stopper molded "Raquel Meller."

R E N A U D / L U B I N (R e l)

Rel-1 Sur Deux Notes Fig. 180

Size: 14 cm   Mark: 15   Rarity: 1   Value: B

U.S. trademark 1947, in use since 1940 by Renaud. Molded "Lalique." One known complete with original box, label, and perfume.

Rel-2 Lubin version of Sur Deux Notes Fig. 180

Size: 24 cm   Mark: 14   Rarity: 1   Value: B

1920. Design apparently made prewar for Lubin and during and/or postwar for Renaud. Molded "RL" and "Lubin."

R O G E R e t G A L L E T (R & G)

R&G-1 Narkiss (a.k.a. Althéa) Fig. 80

Size: 9 cm   Mark: 14   Rarity: 2   Value: B

1910s. Flower in center with enamel.

R&G-2 Paquerettes Fig. 91

Size: 8 cm   Mark: 15   Rarity: 1   Value: A +

1910s. Tiara with daisy design.

R&G-3 Le Jade Fig. 96

Size: 8 cm   Mark: 8 and 14   Rarity: 3   Value: A/B

1920s. Also, there are elaborate Le Jade winged bird cardboard boxes and aluminum powder boxes with same design, signed "R. Lalique."

R&G-4 Pavots d'Argent Fig. 97

Size: 8 cm   Mark: 8   Rarity: 3/4   Value: C
11 cm

1926. Powder box to match, in cardboard.

R&G-5 Flausa Fig. 94

Size: 12 cm   Mark: 15   Rarity: 1   Value: A +

1910s. Design of robed girl in mold. Molded "Flausa" on front and "Roger et Gallet" on reverse. Signature on stopper. Collection Marie-Claude Lalique. A mint example, sealed and complete with original label and packaging sold for $30,000 in Paris in 1989.

R&G-6 Cigalia Fig. 89

Size: 9 cm   Mark: NS   Rarity: 1   Value: A/B
12.5 cm
18.5 cm

1911. Pressed-wood box. 4 Cicadas design. Three sizes.

R&G-7 Salvia Fig. 92

Size: 11 cm   Mark: UK   Rarity: 1   Value: B

Items 7 and 8 seen in photos in *La Renaissance de l'Art Français et des Industries de Luxe,* p. 30, 1919 and in Roger et Gallet 1920s catalog.

R&G-8 Psyka Fig. 93

Size: 10 cm   Mark: NS   Rarity: 1   Value: B

See above comments. Butterfly label and box design.

R&G-9 Rose Rouge (a.k.a. Rosebuds) Fig. 95

Size: 11 cm   Mark: 15   Rarity: 2   Value: B/C
intaglio

1910s. Rosebuds on edge of bottle.

R&G-10 Persana Fig. 127

Size: 14 cm   Mark: NS   Rarity: 1   Value: C

1910s. Same bottle and "flame" stopper as Fragonard (Fr-1).

Note: Roger et Gallet is now part of Sanofi-France. Roger et Gallet was Lalique's second client for commercial perfume bottles.

R O S I N E (R o s)

Ros-1 Nuit de Chine Fig. 127

Size: 8 cm   Mark: 9   Rarity: 1/2   Value: C

1913. Flame stopper. Flask with elongated neck. Also see Fragonard. Fragonard and Rosine perfume brands closely allied with House of Poiret.

R O T T E R D A M L L O Y D (R L)

RL-1 Royal Dutch Mail Fig. 245

Size: 10 cm   Mark: 1   Rarity: 1   Value: C

Cactus (ML-519), but marked "Royal Dutch Mail— Rotterdam Lloyd" as limited issue.

S A K S F I F T H A V E N U E (S a k s)

Saks-1 Trésor de la Mer Fig. 213, 214

Size: 10 cm h.   Mark: 1   Rarity: 1   Value: A +
14 cm w.

1939 Lalique Exhibition at Saks Fifth Avenue. Opal shell box with pearl-shaped perfume insert. Fifty made in commemoration of fifty-year anniversary of Saks New York. Only one complete set known. Original working name was *Coquille Amerique.*

T O K A L O N (T o)

To-1 Petalia (a.k.a. Captivant de Tokalon) Fig. 201

Size: 11.5 cm   Mark: 8   Rarity: 1   Value: A +

U.S. trademark 1925. Sunburst face.

VEOLAY (Veo)

Veo-1 Niobe Violet Fig. 196

Size: 11 cm   Mark: 14   Rarity: 1   Value: A

Introduced into the U.S. in 1928. Birds applied to shoulders of bottle.

VOLNAY (Vo)

Vo-1 Gros Fruits—Volnay Fig. 170

Size: 13.5 cm   Mark: 8   Rarity: 1   Value: A

Same as *Gros Fruits* for Maison Lalique (ML-501), except has "Volnay Paris" in mold. Collection Marie-Claude Lalique.

Vo-2 Jasmin de Cap Fig. 171

Size: 8.5 cm   Mark: 8   Rarity: 3/4   Value: C

Square flask, and stopper with *Épines* design. Usually stained brown.

Vo-3 Volnais (a.k.a. Chypre) Fig. 171

Size: 12 cm   Mark: 8   Rarity: 2   Value: B

Oval flask, flowers and vines design with conical stopper. Brown stain. Stopper molded "Volnay Paris."

Vo-4 Square section Fig. 172

Size: 12 cm   Mark: 8   Rarity: 1   Value: B

Frosted *Épines* design. Collection Marie-Claude Lalique. Also seen with thinner stopper.

Vo-5 Jardinée Fig. 174

Size: 12.5 cm   Mark: 7   Rarity: 3   Value: B/C

Brown stain. Flower heads design. Circular flask.

Vo-6 Gri-Gri Fig. 173

Size: 9.5 cm   Mark: 10   Rarity: 1/2   Value: A/B

1921. Heart shape. Coral pattern.

WORTH (W)

W-1 to W-5 Dans la Nuit (and variations)

Size: Various   Mark: Various
Rarity: 1 to 6   Value: A to E

Basic Models:

W-1 Spherical globe (1924) Fig. 15, 134
W-2 Flat round flask (1924) Fig. 130, 133, 138, 153, 239
W-3 Flat round with chevron design all over (1927) Fig. 129
W-4 Flat round with chevron design on top half (1929)
W-5 Crescent flask with chevron design (also an atomizer version) Fig. 129
W-3, 4, and 5 for Vers le Jour.

Decorative and Color Variations:

W-1 A—Clear with molded stars
W-1 B—Clear without molded stars
W-1 C—With blue enamel and molded stars

(Glass Colors)

W-2 A—Cobalt blue Generally for Dans la Nuit.
W-2 B—Medium blue Generally for Je Reviens.
W-2 C—Clear Generally for cologne/lotion.
W-2 D—Orange Generally for Vers le Jour.
W-2 E—Green Generally for Sans Adieu.
W-2 F—Orange center, clear edges Generally for Vers le Jour.
W-2 G—Turquoise

(Vers le Jour)

W-3, W-4, W-5 A—Orange
W-3, W-4, W-5 B—Orange/amber center shading to green edges
W-3, W-4, W-5 C—Orange/amber center shading to clear edges
W-3, W-4, W-5 D—Dark amber center shading to orange edges

Stoppers (Colors Match Bottle):

A—Upright flat round with "Dans la Nuit"
B—Upright flat round with "W"
C—Upright flat round with quarter moon and stars
D—Upright flat round with chevron pattern ★
E—Upright flat round plain and clear ★
F—With metal stopper
G—With green stopper like Sans Adieu
H—With turquoise stopper like Je Reviens (button ★)
I—With turquoise stopper like Je Reviens (ribbed) postwar only. (Older in glass, later in plastic ★)
★ Also seen with "dauber" stem into bottle.

Introduced 1920s. Pre-1945 signed "R. Lalique," postwar "Lalique." Je Reviens presented in many *Dans la Nuit* bottle and stopper designs. Also Vers Toi, Sans Adieu, Projets, Vers le Jour, and Imprudence were made in versions of body models W-2, W-3, and W-4. Rarity/Value: From 6-E to 1-A. The most common are body Model W-1 without enamel and body model W-2 in clear or in the smaller medium blue versions. The medium value/rarity group includes body model W-1 with blue enamel and body model W-2 in cobalt blue glass. The most valuable are (1) the body types W-3, W-4, and W-5, (2) the orange, green, and exotic glass colors, and (3) any body style/color with stoppers such as Sans Adieu, Je Reviens, and Imprudence. Prewar models are, of course more valuable than postwar. Small (7 cm) medium blue flask with button stopper (molded "R. Lalique") seen with ivy design etched on face of bottle and "12/46" etched on base. Prior to 1936, the stoppers with quarter moon and stars (C) were used. Procter & Gamble (U.S.) objected to protect its logo for Ivory soap and Worth changed to stopper styles A and B. Body models W-1 and W-2 reintroduced 1985 molded "Creation Lalique."

W-6 Je Reviens Fig. 131

Size: 6 cm to 29 cm   Mark: 9   Rarity: 3/5   Value: B to E

Introduced 1932. Blue glass. Four sizes. Usually with turquoise button stopper prewar and ribbed stopper postwar. Postwar without "R."

W-7 Imprudence Fig. 134

Size: 7.5 cm 10 cm 14 cm   Mark: 9   Rarity: 4   Value: C/D

Introduced 1938. Usually with circular stopper prewar and square stopper postwar. Sometimes with silver trim on edges. Three sizes. Postwar without "R."

W-8 Sans Adieu Fig. 133

Size: 5 cm to 14 cm   Mark: 9   Rarity: 3/4   Value: C

Introduced 1929, also postwar. Green glass. Three sizes. Postwar without "R."

W-9 Lilas (a.k.a. Daisies) Fig. 137

Size: 7 cm to 13 cm   Mark: 8   Rarity: 4/5   Value: D

Late 1930s. Various stains. Four sizes.

W-10 Projets (a.k.a. Clear Sailing) Fig. 136

Size: 4.5 cm 7 cm 9 cm   Mark: 9   Rarity: 3   Value: C

Introduced into U.S. in 1936. Clear. Three sizes.

W-11 Vers Toi (a.k.a. Pot de Fleurs) Fig. 135

Size: 4.5 cm to   Mark: 10   Rarity: 3   Value: C/D
18 cm

Introduced into U.S. in 1933. Clear. Three sizes.

W-12 Egg shape Fig. 139

Size: 5.5 cm   Mark: 9   Rarity: 1   Value: A/B

Frosted with stylized "W" design. Collection Marie-Claude Lalique. 1929.

Note: Stoppers for *Je Reviens* (W-6) and *Imprudence* (W-7) were redesigned in 1952 by Marc Lalique. Je Reviens changed from button stopper to ribbed stopper and Imprudence changed from circular to square.

M A N U F A C T U R E R
U N K N O W N (U K)

UK-1 Lierre Fig. 206

Size: 11.5 cm   Mark: 7   Rarity: 3   Value: C/D
16 cm

Tapering rectangular section, floral stopper.

UK-2 Joined rectangular sections Fig. 207

Size: 12 cm   Mark: 5   Rarity: 1   Value: A+

Two compartments. Separate bird-design stoppers. Collection Marie-Claude Lalique.

UK-3 Circular flask Fig. 200

Size: 8.5 cm   Mark: 8   Rarity: 1   Value: A

Leaves and flowers decoration.

UK-4 Oval flask and pointed stopper Fig. 200

Size: 11 cm   Mark: 10   Rarity: 1   Value: A

Frosted bands of birds and berries.

UK-5 Clear center with frosted sides Fig. 185

Size: 11 cm   Mark: 8   Rarity: 1   Value: B

Flared sides with draped design. Collection Marie-Claude Lalique.

UK-6 Six-sided flask Fig. 185

Size: 7.5 cm   Mark: 8   Rarity: 1   Value: B/C

Beading decoration on edges of base, disk stopper, and oval panel in center.

UK-7 Octagonal flask Fig. 223

Size: 6 cm   Mark: 8   Rarity: 1   Value: A+

Black enamel design of stylized flowers. Pyramid stopper. Collection Marie-Claude Lalique.

UK-8 Small tapered cylinder Fig. 216

Size: 6.5 cm   Mark: 9   Rarity: 1   Value: A/B

Overlapping petal design. Collection Musée International de la Parfumerie, Grasse, France.

UK-9 Triangular flask Fig. 186

Size: 13 cm   Mark: NS   Rarity: 1   Value: A

Fern leaf design on sides and pointed stopper. Possibly for Lubin (see Rel-2) as decoration is similar. Collection Marie-Claude Lalique.

E X P E R I M E N T A L
M O D E L S (E X)

EX-1 Demilune base with blue carnation motif Fig. 81

Size: 10 cm   Mark: 3

Blue liquid coloring. Collection Marie-Claude Lalique. *Lalique par Lalique,* EDIPOP, Lausanne, 1977, page 213. A second example has recently been identified.

EX-2 Eagle frieze Fig. 7

Size: 12.5 cm   Mark: NS

Collection Marie-Claude Lalique. Vase of same design, *Lalique par Lalique,* EDIPOP, Lausanne, 1977, page 185.

EX-3 Square section with fish heads at corners Fig. 9

Size: 11 cm   Mark: NS

Clear disk stopper. Collection Marie-Claude Lalique. *Lalique par Lalique,* EDIPOP, Lausanne, 1977, page 213. Similar to Cigales (ML-475).

EX-4 Circular flask with amber inset of two nudes Fig. 10

Size: 10 cm   Mark: NS

Collection Marie-Claude Lalique.

EX-5 Ovoid flask with concave center Fig. 88

Size: 11 cm   Mark: NS

Same as ML-17 except larger, with slightly different body shape and stopper. Collection Marie-Claude Lalique.

EX-6 Same as prior except square flask Fig. 11

Size: 8.5 cm   Mark: NS

Stopper of conical shape, from stock (de Vigny's *Jamerose* [deV-2]). Collection Marie-Claude Lalique.

EX-7 Cigalia in green Fig. 12

Size: 12.5 cm   Mark: NS

Experimental color of Roger et Gallet model (R&G-6). Collection Marie-Claude Lalique.

EX-8 Silver Serpent Fig. 16

Size: 6 cm   Mark: NS

1898–99. Agate and silver. Reference 1682, Sigrid Barten, *René Lalique: Schmuck und Objets d'Art 1890–1910* (Munich: Prestel-Verlag, 1977). Collection Musée des Arts Décoratifs, Paris.

EX-9 Amethyst Fig. 14

Size: 6 cm   Mark: NS

1896. Rock crystal, enamel, silver and amethyst. Reference 1680, Barten (above). Collection Musée des Arts Décoratifs, Paris.

EX-10 Masque eau de toilette Fig. 13

Size: 25.5 cm   Mark: 3

Circa 1910. See Figure 17 in Nicholas M. Dawes, *Lalique Glass* (New York: Crown Publishers, 1986), p. 14. Phillips, 10/6/79, Lot 154.

EX-11 *Cire-perdue* teardrop with fish Fig. 3

Size: 10 cm   Mark: NS

Reputedly the first glass perfume bottle by René Lalique. *Cire-perdue* process. Circa 1893. Collection Lillian Nassau. Phillips, February 9, 1980, Lot 168. Provenance: René Lalique, Marc Lalique, Elie Khourie of A. N. Khourie & Bros., Robert L. Zrike. Exhibition: The Louvre, Paris, 1925–45. A second example surfaced in Paris in late 1988.

Post-1945 Production
Marc Lalique and Marie-Claude Lalique

LANCÔME (Lan)

Lan-101 Magie (a.k.a. Baton de Magicien) Fig. 231

Size: 12.5 cm   Mark: NS
Available Prewar: No   Rarity: 4   Value: D/E

1952. Stars decoration. Came in a suede pouch. Designed by Marc Lalique.

Lan-102 Sphère Magie Fig. 231

Size: 4 cm   Mark: NS
Available Prewar: No   Rarity: 3   Value: D/E

Gold-plated dome; star-studded decoration. Designed by Marc Lalique.

Lan-103 Jumeles Fig. 232

Size: 11 cm   Mark: NS
Available Prewar: No   Rarity: 2   Value: D/E

Two tubular frosted bottles with gold-plated metal screw stoppers. Sold as a set. Bases angled and tubes notched so they lean together. Designed by Marc Lalique.

Lan-104 Marrakech Fig. 230

Size: 13.5 cm   Mark: M
Available Prewar: No   Rarity: 1   Value: A/B

1946. Vase/carafe shape with flared design on sides. First and probably best Marc Lalique design for Lancôme.

MARCEL ROCHAS (Ro)

Ro-101 Femme (a.k.a. La Rose and Mouche) Fig. 233

Size: 9 cm to 18 cm   Mark: SB
Available Prewar: No   Rarity: 5   Value: D/E

Designed 1943. Some signed—most not. Some slightly different shapes (oval base versus round base). Designed by Marc Lalique.

Ro-102 La Rose Fig. 234

Size: 21.5 cm   Mark: SB
Available Prewar: No   Rarity: 3   Value: C

1945 design. Floral center. Same basic design as C-117 *(Moulin Rouge)* but with different ornamentation and stopper. Designed by Marc Lalique.

MOLINARD (M)

M-101 Calendal (a.k.a. Bacchantes) Fig. 161

Size: 11.5 cm   Mark: E and SB
Available Prewar: Yes   Rarity: 4   Value: B/C

Same as prewar (M-2) except signature. Made until early 1950s. Designed by René Lalique.

M-102 Madrigal Fig. 162

Size: 15 cm   Mark: E
Available Prewar: Yes   Rarity: 2/3   Value: B/C

Same as prewar (M-3) except signature. Made until early 1950s. Designed by René Lalique.

M-103 Les Îles d'Or Fig. 163

Size: 11 cm   Mark: E
Available Prewar: Yes   Rarity: 2   Value: B

Same as prewar (M-4) except signature. Made until early 1950s. Designed by René Lalique.

M-104 Molinard de Molinard Fig. 163

Size: 8.5 cm, 11 cm   Mark: M
Available Prewar: Yes   Rarity: 6   Value: E

New mold 1980s. Signed in mold "Creation Lalique." Same as prewar (M-4) and postwar (M-103) *Les Îles d'Or,* except mold clarity, crispness, and signature. Designed by René Lalique.

MORABITO (Mor)

Mor-101 No 7 (a.k.a. Tortues) Fig. 135

Size: 11 cm, 14 cm, 22 cm   Mark: SB
Available Prewar: No   Rarity: 2   Value: A

1951. Turtle design in amber/orange glass. Three sizes. Designed by Marc Lalique.

NINA RICCI (NR)

NR-101 Fille d'Eve (A) Fig. 242

Size: 6 cm to 14 cm   Mark: E
Available Prewar: No   Rarity: 3/4   Value: D/E

1952. Apple with leaf stopper. Three different leaf designs. Four sizes. Designed by Marc Lalique.

NR-102 Fille d'Eve (B) Fig. 242

Size: 4 cm, 6 cm   Mark: SB
Available Prewar: No   Rarity: 3/4   Value: D/E

1950s. Apple-shaped flask. Gold-plated stopper. Two purse sizes with suede case. Designed by Marc Lalique.

NR-103 Coeur Joie (A) Fig. 235, 240

Size: 9 cm to 15 cm   Mark: SB/E
Available Prewar: No   Rarity: 5   Value: D/E

Designed 1942. Heart shape with open center. Four sizes. Designed by Marc Lalique.

NR-104 Coeur Joie (B) Fig. 243

Size: 6 cm to 21 cm   Mark: M
Available Prewar: No   Rarity: 5   Value: D/E

Introduced 1951. "NR" molded on neck of flask. Perfume Capricci also in this bottle. Five sizes. Designed by Marc Lalique.

NR-105 Coeur Joie (C) Fig. 237

Size: 10 cm to 18 cm   Mark: M
Available Prewar: No   Rarity: 3   Value: D/E

Designed 1943. Flask with long neck and "NR" molding. Three sizes. Designed by Marc Lalique.

NR-106 Coeur Joie (D), Fig. 148, 240

Size: 4 cm to 9 cm   Mark: M
Available Prewar: No   Rarity: 3   Value: D/E

1950s. "Hearts" vial with pouch cover. Four versions—four-heart, three-heart, two-heart, and one-heart sizes. Designed by Marc Lalique.

NR-107 Capricci Fig. 235

Size: 9 cm to 16 cm   Mark: SB
Available Prewar: No   Rarity: 3   Value: D/E

1961. Cut-glass look. Three sizes. Designed by Marc Lalique.

NR-108 Farouche Fig. 235

Size: 9 cm, 13 cm   Mark: E
Available Prewar: No   Rarity: 4   Value: D/E

1974. Frosted wings. Two sizes. Designed by Marc Lalique.

NR-109 Fleur de Fleurs Fig. 235

Size: 11 cm, 16 cm   Mark: M
Available Prewar: No   Rarity: 4   Value: D/E

1982. Flower head intaglio. Designed by Marie-Claude Lalique.

NR-110 L'Air du Temps (A) (a.k.a. Soleil) Fig. 236

Size: 4 cm to 8 cm   Mark: M
Available Prewar: No   Rarity: 3   Value: D/E

1940s. Gold plastic screw-on stopper. Base with sunburst design to scalloped edges. First Lalique bottle for L'Air du Temps. Three sizes. Designed by Marc Lalique.

NR-111 L'Air du Temps (B) Fig. 238

Size: 10 cm   Mark: M
Available Prewar: No   Rarity: 3   Value: E

Early 1950s. Gold plastic screw-on stopper. Base with fluted waves shape. Designed by Marc Lalique.

NR-112 L'Air du Temps (C) Fig. 239

Size: Various   Mark: M
Available Prewar: No   Rarity: 5   Value: D/E

1950s. Flask. Capricci and Farouche in same bottle. Designed by Marc Lalique.

NR-113 L'Air du Temps (D) (a.k.a. Flacon aux Colombes) Fig. 235, 236, 241

Size: 5 cm to 32 cm   Mark: E
Available Prewar: No   Rarity: 6   Value: C/E

Designed 1947. Four sizes. Available with one or two doves. Miniature size (5 cm) with gold-metal dove stopper and gold-mesh bottle holder. Adaptations of the doves design introduced in 1986 include an oval- and a pear-shaped bottle with doves intaglio on the face of the flask. Designed by Marc Lalique.

NR-114 L'Air du Temps (E) Fig. 239

Size: 5 cm   Mark: NS
Available Prewar: No   Rarity: 4   Value: E

Dove in gold enamel on small oval flask with gold-plated plastic stopper. Designed by Marc Lalique.

NR-115 Bigarade (a.k.a. Signoricci I) Fig. 219

Size: 10.5 cm   Mark: M
Available Prewar: No   Rarity: 3   Value: D/E

1945–50. Oval cylinder with ribs and plastic gold screw-on stopper. Designed by Marc Lalique.

NR-116 Nina (a.k.a. Drape) Fig. 235

Size: Various   Mark: NS
Available Prewar: No   Rarity: 6   Value: E

Introduced 1987. Asymmetrical glass veil. Designed by Marie-Claude Lalique.

RAPHAEL (R)

R-101 Réplique Fig. 148

Size: 5 cm   Mark: E
Available Prewar: No   Rarity: 4   Value: C

Acorn pendant designed early 1940s. Designed by Marc Lalique.

WORTH (W)

W-101 Je Reviens Fig. 131

Size: 6 cm to 29 cm   Mark: M
Available Prewar: Yes   Rarity: 6   Value: C/E

1950s. Same as prewar except usually with ribbed stopper. Blue glass. See W-6. Designed by René Lalique.

W-102 Le Voyageur Fig. 228

Size: 4.5 cm   Mark: M
Available Prewar: No   Rarity: 4   Value: E

Purse size with suede pouch. For ⅛ ounce of Je Reviens, Dans la Nuit or Requête. Metal stopper. Designed by Marc Lalique.

W-103 Dans la Nuit (A) Fig. 15, 134

Size: Various   Mark: Various
Available Prewar: Yes   Rarity: 5   Value: C/E

Sphere (1946–55). With and without blue enamel, etc. Same as Prewar W-1 except for signature without "R." Designed by René Lalique.

1985 Reissue ("Creation Lalique")

Size: Various   Mark: M
Available Prewar: Yes   Rarity: 6   Value: E

Designed by René Lalique.

W-104 Dans la Nuit (B) Fig. 15

Size: Various   Mark: Various
Available Prewar: Yes   Rarity: 6   Value: C/E

1950s. Clear/cobalt blue, etc., circular flask without chevrons. Same as prewar W-2 except for signature without "R." Designed by René Lalique.

1985 Reissue ("Creation Lalique")

Size: Various   Mark: M
Available Prewar: Yes   Rarity: 6   Value: E

Designed by René Lalique. Cobalt blue.

W-105 Requête Fig. 226

Size: 7.5 cm to 29 cm   Mark: M&SB
Available Prewar: No   Rarity: 4   Value: B/D

Designed by Marc Lalique in late 1944. Produced postwar. Blue enamel. Four sizes.

W-106 Sans Adieu Fig. 133

Size: 5 cm to 14 cm   Mark: M
Available Prewar: Yes   Rarity: 4   Value: C/D

Green glass. Made pre- and postwar. See W-8. Signature without "R." Designed by René Lalique.

146

W-107 Imprudence Fig. 227

Size: 7.5 cm to 14 cm   Mark: SB
Available Prewar: Yes   Rarity: 4/5   Value: D

1950s. Same as prewar except usually with square stopper and signature without "R." See W-7. Designed by René Lalique.

C R I S T A L   L A L I Q U E
(C L)

CL-101 Fleurs Concaves Fig. 53

Size: 12 cm   Mark: SB
Available Prewar: Yes   Rarity: 2   Value: C

See ML-486 prewar. Same except signatures. Designed by René Lalique.

CL-102 Salamandres Fig. 36

Size: 9.5 cm   Mark: SB
Available Prewar: Yes   Rarity: 2   Value: C

See ML-491 prewar. Same except signature. Designed by René Lalique.

CL-103 Cactus ** Fig. 245

Size: 10 cm, 12 cm   Mark: E
Available Prewar: Yes   Rarity: 6   Value: D

Designed 1928. Catalog numbers 11365 and 11366. Also see ML-519 prewar. Designed by René Lalique.

CL-104 Clairefontaine ** Fig. 65

Size: 12 cm   Mark: E
Available Prewar: Yes   Rarity: 5   Value: D

Designed 1931. Catalog number 11300. Also see ML-526 prewar. Designed by René Lalique.

CL-105 Dahlia ** Fig. 247

Size: 9 cm to 21 cm   Mark: E
Available Prewar: Yes   Rarity: 6   Value: D

Catalog number 11350. Also see ML-615 prewar. Four sizes. Designed by René Lalique.

CL-106 Duncan ** Fig. 244

Size: 20 cm   Mark: SB/E
Available Prewar: Yes   Rarity: 5   Value: D

Originally designed 1931 and sold immediately postwar with "Lalique" signature. Catalog numbers 11380 and 11381. See ML-623 prewar. Four sizes. Reintroduction of two sizes in 1974 with modified stopper by Marc Lalique. Designed by René Lalique and Marc Lalique.

CL-107 Enfants ** Fig. 246

Size: 10 cm   Mark: E
Available Prewar: Yes   Rarity: 5   Value: D

Designed 1930. Catalog number 11363. ML-609 prewar also. Designed by René Lalique.

CL-108 Deux Fleurs (a.k.a. Deux Marguerites) ** Fig. 80

Size: 8.5 cm   Mark: E
Available Prewar: Yes   Rarity: 5   Value: D

Designed 1935–36. Catalog number 11301. Also see ML-1 prewar. Designed by René Lalique.

CL-109 Hélène Fig. 248

Size: 14 cm, 22.5 cm   Mark: E
Available Prewar: Yes   Rarity: 4   Value: C/D

Made until 1950s. Large version with two rows of four panels. Also prewar (ML-2). Designed by René Lalique.

CL-110 Rosace Figurines Fig. 94

Size: 13 cm   Mark: E
Available Prewar: Yes   Rarity: 1   Value: A/B

Two nymphs stopper design as on 1950s stemware by Marc Lalique. Two known with gold-enamel finish. Same as ML-488 except with two nymphs stopper and signature. Designed by René Lalique and Marc Lalique.

CL-111 Floride ** Fig. 251

Size: 16 cm   Mark: E
Available Prewar: No   Rarity: 4   Value: D

Designed 1956. Catalog number 11374. Designed by Marc Lalique.

CL-112 St. Germain Fig. 249

Size: 10 cm   Mark: E
Available Prewar: No   Rarity: 3   Value: C/D

Eight-sided. Catalog number 11371. Discontinued some years ago. Designed by Marc Lalique.

CL-113 Robinson ** Fig. 250

Size: 11 cm   Mark: E
Available Prewar: No   Rarity: 4   Value: D

Designed 1946. Sixteen-sided. Catalog number 11368. Designed by Marc Lalique.

CL-114 Martine ** Fig. 252

Size: 14.5 cm   Mark: E
Available Prewar: No   Rarity: 4   Value: D

Catalog number 11202. Designed by Marc Lalique.

CL-115 Cassiopée Fig. 255

Size: 19 cm, 22.5 cm   Mark: E
Available Prewar: No   Rarity: 3   Value: C/D

Designed 1963. Catalog numbers 11376 and 11377. Recently discontinued. Designed by Marie-Claude Lalique.

CL-116 Pomme ** Fig. 254

Size: 13 cm   Mark: E
Available Prewar: No   Rarity: 5   Value: D

Created in 1952 as *Fille d'Eve* (NR-101) for Nina Ricci. Catalog number 11646. Reintroduced for Cristal Lalique in one size only, in 1976. Designed by Marc Lalique.

CL-117 Moulin Rouge ** Fig. 253

Size: 17.5 cm   Mark: E
Available Prewar: No   Rarity: 4   Value: D

See Rochas' *La Rose* (Ro-102). Same basic design but with different decoration, stopper, and height. Catalog number 11304. Designed by Marc Lalique.

CL-118 Samoa ** Fig. 256

Size: 8 cm   Mark: E
Available Prewar: No   Rarity: 5   Value: D

Designed 1979. Catalog number 11312. Designed by Marie-Claude Lalique.

CL-119 Baptiste ** Fig. 257

Size: 7.5 cm   Mark: E
Available Prewar: No   Rarity: 5   Value: D

Designed 1979. Catalog number 11313. Designed by Marie-Claude Lalique.

Note: ** All information courtesy Cristal Lalique, Paris. ** Currently available (1988). Also, three new designs by Marie-Claude Lalique were introduced in 1989.

NOTES

CHAPTER 1

1. Marc and Marie-Claude Lalique, *Lalique par Lalique* (Paris: Société Lalique, 1977), p. 20.

2. Vivienne Becker, *The Jewellery of René Lalique* (London: Goldsmiths' Company, 1987), p. 16.

3. The style's name came from S. Bing's Paris shop, La Maison de l'Art Nouveau. Siegfried Bing— long known as Samuel Bing—was an important patron of Lalique and featured the goldsmith's pieces in his shops and exhibition displays.

4. *René Lalique, Sculptor in Glass* (New York: B. Altman and Company, 1935).

5. An almost identical *cire perdue* flacon, but with a gold cover over the stopper and signed Lalique in the metal, was sold to the Musée D'Orsay (Paris) for over $50,000 at a Paris auction June 22, 1988. (Ader Picard Tajan sale from the estate of Nina Alexandrovna Konchine, Lot 8.) Experts Félix Marcilhac and Jean-Marc Maury placed the date of this piece as circa 1905. The relationship between this piece and the illustrated example has not been established.

6. This information comes from a Chronologie– René Lalique compiled by Félix Marcilhac, which is included in the exposition catalog *René Lalique: Maître-Verrier,* Tokyo Metropolitan Teien Art Museum, April-May 1988, The Asahi Shimbun, Tokyo.

7. Lalique's oldest child, Suzanne (b. 1892), a noted stage-set designer, married into the Haviland porcelain firm of Limoges, for whom she designed ceramics. She was also a painter who resided in the French countryside until her death in April 1989.

CHAPTER 2

1. Quoted in C.J.S. Thompson, *The Mystery and Lure of Perfume* (London: John Lane/The Bodley Head Limited, 1927), p. 91.

2. *Ibid.,* p. 96.

3. *Ibid.,* p. 97.

4. Kate Foster, *Scent Bottles* (London: The Connoisseur and Michael Joseph, 1966), p. 13.

5. Patrick Süskind, *Perfume: The Story of a Murderer,* trans. John E. Woods (Harmondsworth, Middlesex: Viking Penguin, 1987), p. 37–38; (New York: Alfred A. Knopf, Inc., 1986).

6. Edmund Launert, *Scent & Scent Bottles* (London: Barrie & Jenkins, 1974), p. 12.

7. *Ibid.*

CHAPTER 3

1. Both are included in Sigrid Barten's volume, *René Lalique: Schmuck und Objets d'Art 1890–1910* (Munich: Prestel-Verlag, 1977), the definitive work

on Lalique's jewels and illustrations as well as actual pieces (*see* numbers 1680, 1682, pp. 537–538).

2. Nicholas M. Dawes, *Lalique Glass* (New York: Crown Publishers, Inc., 1986), p. 13.

3. Philippa Warburg, "Beginning with Lalique," *Hobbies,* September 1980, p. 52.

4. See press release "The Story of Coty," New York, circa 1986.

5. Mr. Vindry related this information to the authors when they visited the Musée de Grasse in January 1988.

6. Gabriel Mourey, "Lalique's Glassware," *Commercial Art,* July 1926, pp. 32, 34.

7. Dawes, *op. cit.,* p. 15.

8. Coty helped other *parfumeurs* as well, albeit indirectly, at one time employing the future founders of Charles of the Ritz, Lancôme, and Orlane.

9. This was the case for other *parfumeurs* as well, who often followed up the success of one of their scents by bottling other fragrances in the same flacon, hoping to ride on the coattails of the first perfume and make the others popular as well.

10. In Margaret Allen's book, *Selling Dreams* (London: J. M. Dent & Sons Ltd., 1981, p. 44), "L'Origin" [*sic*] by Coty is mentioned as "the oldest-surviving of twentieth-century perfumes." There are, of course, eaux de cologne, such as 4711 and Jean-Marie Farina, dating from much earlier times.

11. Gustave Kahn, "Lalique Verrier," *Art et Décoration,* January–June 1912, vol. 31, p. 155; English translation by the authors.

12. Dawes, *op. cit.,* p. 16.

13. Available today in reprint form (New York: Dover Press, 1982). A handsome facsimile version is available from Galerie Moderne in London.

14. These lamps are not pictured in the 1932 catalog, but many appear in vintage brochures put out by Breves Galleries in London.

15. This information comes from an article by Souren Melikian in the *International Herald-Tribune,* January 30–31, 1988. One can assume Mr. Melikian received these detailed descriptions from Lalique expert Félix Marcilhac, who organized the auction of Lalique glass in Paris that is featured in the article and who is the author of an imminent *catalogue raisonné* of Lalique's works.

16. Barten, *op. cit.,* p. 25.

1. Nicholas M. Dawes, *Lalique Glass* (New York: Crown Publishers, Inc., 1986), p. 17.

2. Gabriel Mourey, "Lalique's Glassware," *Commercial Art,* July 1926, p. 34.

3. Maximilien Gauthier, "Le Maître Verrier René Lalique à l'Exposition," *La Renaissance de l'Art Français et des Industries de Luxe,* September 1925, p. 415.

4. *L'Exposition des Arts Décoratifs et Industriels Modernes Rapport Général* (Parfumerie, Section Française), September 1925. Quoted in Dawes, *op. cit.,* p. 60.

5. Henri Clouzot, "Le Flaconnage Artistique Moderne," *La Renaissance de l'Art Francais et des Industries de Luxe,* January 1919, pp. 31–32.

6. From Jean-Claude Ellena, "Les Mots du Parfum," *Air France Atlas,* October 1987, p. 148.

7. Several sheets of data on Roger et Gallet were presented by Mr. Davy to the authors on a visit to Bernay in January 1988.

8. As the article in *La Renaissance de l'Art Français et des Industries de Luxe,* September 1922, points out, all the top couturiers, modistes, *parfumeurs,* tailors, jewelers, art dealers, and others were situated on or near the Rue de la Paix, Place Vendôme, and Rue de Castiglione in 1920s Paris (the equivalent of New Bond Street in London or upper Madison Avenue in Manhattan). Within that stretch, extending from the Rue de Rivoli to the Opéra, were Lalique, Coty, Roger et Gallet, Arys, Guerlain, Worth, and D'Orsay, as well as the Hotel Ritz, the Louis Sherry *confiserie* (confectionery shop), the art-dealer brothers Duveen, Bankers Trust, and Tiffany & Co.

9. Perhaps the alternate name of Parfums D'Orsay, La Compagnie Française des Parfums, was chosen to form a link between it and Süe et Mare's similarly named establishment.

10. A photograph in Guillaume Janneau's article, "Le Mouvement Moderne: La Maison du Chevalier D'Orsay," *La Renaissance de l'Art Français et des Industries de Luxe,* March 1927, p. 138, features a display of chiefly black-glass bottles, which lends credence to this observation.

11. *La Parfumerie Française dans l'Art et la Présentation* (Paris: 1925).

149

12. Formerly men had not been involved with designing ladies' clothes. Instead, they were haberdashers, tailors, and the like. Worth changed all that, however.

13. In general, fragrances have three basic components, each with a differing evaporation level: the top, or head note, is the volatile one; the middle, or body, can be powerful or light; and the bottom note, the foundation, underlines and stresses the scent and is essentially its "memory."

14. The authors are grateful to Georges Bonnemaison of Worth for this interesting anecdote, which was related to them while on a visit to Worth's facilities in early 1988.

15. .There was also a very large spherical Dans la Nuit flacon, *Boulle Majestique,* which was named after the Majestic Hotel in Cannes, opened in 1925 around the time of the scent's introduction.

16. Jean-Yves Gaborit, *Perfumes: The Essences and Their Bottles* (New York: Rizzoli International, 1985), p. 156.

17. According to Diana De Marly in her book *Worth, Father of Haute Couture* (London: Elm Tree Books, 1980), p. 209, *chic* was "a new term which [Worth] made fashionable as early as 1860, meaning, in the words of one of his customers, 'personal elegance, elegance having a look.' "

18. An architectural reference was made, too, in a 1938 American magazine, *Toliet Requisites,* which wrote that Lalique had "built a little glass castle, each tier banded with silver, in which to house this warm, joyous scent."

19. *Molinard,* catalog marking the 100th aniversary of the firm (Montrouge/Seine): Draeger Frères, 1949), p. 7 (book unpaginated).

20. Vintage advertisement reproduced in Jacquelyne Y. Jones-North, *Commercial Perfume Bottles* (West Chester, Pa: Schiffer Publishing Ltd., 1987), p. 189.

21. According to Jacquelyne Y. Jones-North, in her book *Perfumes, Colognes and Scent Bottles* (West Chester, Pa: Schiffer Publishing Ltd., 1986, p. 40), the heads "match figures on the portico of the Guerlain building in Paris."

22. This according to Georges Vindry of the Musée Internationale de la Parfumerie in Grasse.

23. The authors would again like to thank Georges Vindry of the Musée Internationale de la Parfumerie in Grasse for this history, related to them on a visit to Grasse in January 1988.

24. The authors are deeply grateful to Cristal Lalique, especially to Odette Boulanger and Catherine Hyden, for allowing us to delve into their archives.

25. The original Institut de Beauté was founded in 1895 by one Madame Valentin Le Brun. Whether Merle's establishment was related to Mme Le Brun's —for example, as a franchise or a branch of her salon —is not known.

26. In the 1950s Parfums Lucien Lelong was absorbed by Coty.

27. A patent application was not filed for this bottle until 1931, even though it had appeared in advertisements in 1930.

28. Our thanks to Mr. Davy for this information, relayed to us in a conversation at Roger et Gallet/ Sanofi headquarters in Bernay, France, in early 1988.

CHAPTER 5

1. Our thanks to Georges Bonnemaison of Worth for this information, related to us in early 1988.

2. From a 1988 Nina Ricci press release titled "Nina Ricci Informations," p. 1 of 3.

3. Nicholas M. Dawes, *Lalique Glass* (New York: Crown Publishers, Inc., 1986), p. 124.

CHAPTER 6

1. Pierre Dinand has designed bottles for Coty's Complice, Loris Azzaro's Azzaro, Yves Saint Laurent's Opium and Y, plus other award-winning bottles for Armani, Balenciaga, Balmain, Caron, Jean Desprez, Givenchy, Missoni, and Molyneux.

BIBLIOGRAPHY

BOOKS ON RENÉ LALIQUE

Arwas, Victor. *Lalique*. New York: Rizzoli International, 1980.

Barten, Sigrid. *René Lalique: Schmuck und Objets d'Art 1890–1910*. Munich: Prestel-Verlag, 1977.

Bayer, Patricia, and Mark Waller. *The Art of René Lalique*. London: Bloomsbury, 1988.

Becker, Vivienne. *The Jewellery of René Lalique*. London: Goldsmiths' Company, 1987.

Bley, Alice. *A Guide to Fraudulent Lalique*. Ohio: Antique Appraisers Association, 1981.

Dawes, Nicholas M. *Lalique Glass*. New York: Crown Publishers, Inc., 1986.

Lalique, Marc, and Marie-Claude Lalique. *Lalique par Lalique*. Paris: Société Lalique, 1977.

Lalique, Marie-Claude. *Lalique*. Geneva: Edipop S.A., 1988.

Lauvrik, Nilsen J. *René Lalique: Master Craftsman*. New York: Haviland and Co., 1912.

McClinton, Katharine Morrison. *An Introduction to Lalique Glass*. Des Moines, Ia: Wallace Homestead, 1978.

————. *Lalique for Collectors*. New York: Scribner's, 1975.

Percy, Christopher Vane. *The Glass of Lalique: A Collector's Guide*. New York: Charles Scribner's Sons, 1978.

MUSEUM, GALLERY, AND AUCTION CATALOGS

B. Altman and Company. *René Lalique: Sculptor in Glass*. New York: B. Altman and Company, 1935.

Breves Galleries. *Lalique Light and Decorations*. London: Breves Galleries, circa 1928.

————. *The Art of René Lalique*. London: Breves Galleries, circa 1930.

————. *Lalique Car Mascots*. London: Breves Galleries, circa 1928.

Fitchburg Art Museum. *René Lalique Glass: The Charles and Mary Magriel Collection*. Fitchburg, Mass.: Fitchburg Art Museum, 1975.

Kahn, Gustave. *Works of René Lalique*. London: Agnew's Gallery, Old Bond St., 1905.

Lalique et Cie. *Catalogue des Verreries de René Lalique*. Paris: Lalique et Cie, 1932. Reprint. New York: Dover Press, 1982.

Museum Bellerive. *René Lalique*. Zurich: Museum Bellerive, 1978.

PARCO Gallery. *René Lalique*. Tokyo: PARCO Gallery, 1982.

Tokyo Metropolitan Teien Art Museum. *René Lalique: Maître-Verrier*. Tokyo: Tokyo Metropolitan Teien Art Museum, 1988.

Auction Catalogs from 1977 to date:
  Bonhams, London
  Christie's, New York, London, and Geneva
  Phillips, New York and London
  Sotheby's, New York, London, and Monaco
  Hôtel Drouot, Paris
  Commissaires Priseurs
    M. Gilles Néret-Minet
    M. Olivier Coutau-Bégarie
    M. Hubert LeBlanc
    M. Ader Picard Tajan
  Experts
    Mme. Régine de Robien
    M. Félix Marcilhac

A SELECTION OF
ARTICLES ON LALIQUE
— ◆ —

"An Interview with Marie-Claude Lalique." *Collector Editions,* Summer 1983, 25.

Armand-Dayot, Madelaine. "Le Maître Verrier René Lalique." *L'Art et les Artistes,* 1933, no. 26, 273–77.

Chavance, René. "M. René Lalique à l'Exposition des Arts Décoratifs." *Mobilier et Décoration d'Intérieur,* May 1925, 30–36.

Demoriane, Hélène. "Verres Signé Lalique." *Connaissance des Arts,* April 1970, 112–17.

Destève, Tristan. "La Maison de René Lalique." *Art et Décoration,* November 1902, 161–66.

Gauthïer, Maximilien. "Le Maître Verrier René Lalique à l'Exposition," *La Renaissance de l'Art Français et des Industries de Luxe,* September 1925, 414–19.

Geffroy, Gustave. "Des Bijoux: à propos de M. René Lalique." *Art et Décoration,* December 1905, 177–88.

Gomes-Ferreira, Maria Theresa. "René Lalique at the Calouste Gulbenkian Museum." *Connoisseur,* 1971, 241–49.

Haraucourt, Edmond. "René Lalique et la Verrerie d'Alsace." *Revue de l'Alsace Française,* August 18, 1923.

Hayot, Monelle. "L'Atelier de René Lalique." *L'Oeil,* March 1977, 22–29.

Humair, Sylviane. "Les Flacons à Parfum de Lalique." *Le Figaro,* October 27, 1986.

Kahn, Gustave. "L'Art de René Lalique." *L'Art et les Artistes,* Spring 1905, 223–26.

———. "Lalique Verrier." *Art et Décoration 31,* 1912, 149–58.

———. "Les Verreries de René Lalique." *L'Art et les Artistes,* Winter 1921, 101–06.

Marx, Roger. "Les Maîtres Décorateurs Français: René Lalique." *Art et Décoration,* June 1899, 13–22.

Melikian, Souren. "Paying the Earth for Lalique's Glass 'Objets.'" *International Herald-Tribune,* January 30–31, 1988, 6.

Mourey, Gabriel. "Lalique's Glassware." *Commercial Art,* July 1926, 32–37.

Olmer, Pierre. "Verreries de René Lalique." *Mobilier et Décoration d'Intérieur,* February/March 1924, 1–7.

Stables, Mrs. Gordon. "Lalique." *Artwork,* May 1927, 33.

Warburg, Philippa. "Beginning with Lalique." *Hobbies,* September 1980, 52–53.

B O O K S   O N   P E R F U M E ,
P E R F U M E   B O T T L E S ,
P A R F U M E U R S
— ◆ —

Compagnie des Cristalleries de Baccarat. *Baccarat: The Perfume Bottles.* Paris: Henri Addor Associes, 1986.

Delbourg-Delphis, Marylene. *Le Sillage des Elégantes, Un Siècle d'Histoire des Parfums.* Paris: J. Clattès (Jean-Claude Lattès), 1983.

Foster, Kate. *Scent Bottles.* London: The Connoisseur and Michael Joseph, 1966.

Gaborit, Jean-Yves. *Perfumes: The Essences and Their Bottles.* New York: Rizzoli International, 1985.

Haarman & Reimer. *The H & R Book of Perfume.* Mount Pleasant, S.C.: Gloess Publishing Co.; and London: Johnson Publications Ltd., 1984. (Part of "The Perfume Set," also including *Fragrance Guide: Feminine Notes, Fragrance Guide: Masculine Notes,* and *Guide to Fragrance Ingredients.*)

Jones-North, Jacquelyn Y. *Perfume, Cologne and Scent Bottles.* West Chester, Pa: Schiffer Publishing Ltd., 1986.

———. *Commercial Perfume Bottles.* West Chester, Pa: Schiffer Publishing Ltd., 1987.

Kaufman, William I. *Perfume.* New York: E.P. Dutton, 1974.

Launert, Edmund. *Scent & Scent Bottles.* London: Barrie & Jenkins, Ltd. 1974.

Le Louvre des Antiquaires. *"Autour du Parfum," du*

152

XVI^c au XIX^c Siècle. Paris: Le Louvre des Antiquaires, 1985.

Martin, H. *A Collection of Figural Perfume and Scent Bottles.* Lancaster, Calif.: Martin and Martin, 1982.

Matthews, Leslie. *The Antiques of Perfumes.* New York: Ed. G. Bell and Sons, 1973.

Molinard. *Molinard.* Montrouge (Seine): Draeger Frères, 1949.

Morris, Edwin T. *Fragrance: The Story of Perfume from Cleopatra to Chanel.* New York: Charles Scribner's Sons, 1984.

Pillivuyt, Ghislaine. *Les Flacons de la Séduction: L'Art du Parfum au XVIII^c Siècle.* Lausanne: La Bibliothèque des Arts, 1985.

Sloan, Jean. *Perfume and Scent Bottle Collecting.* Lombard, Ill.: Wallace-Homestead Book Company, 1986.

Süskind, Patrick. *Perfume: The Story of a Murderer.* Translated by John E. Woods. Harmondsworth, Middlesex: Viking Penguin, 1987.

Thompson, C.J.S. *The Mystery and Lure of Perfume.* London: John Lane/The Bodley Head Limited, 1927.

Vindry, Georges. *3000 Ans de Parfumerie* (catalogue l'Exposition de Grasse), July–October 1980.

ARTICLES ON PERFUME, AND PERFUME BOTTLES

◆

Cannell, David. "Fragrance as an Art Form, Part II, The Florals." *Beauty Fashion,* October 1981, 40–48.

———. "Fragrance as an Art Form, Part III, All That Jazz." *Beauty Fashion,* November 1981, 72–78.

———. "Fragrance as an Art Form, Part IV, Art Moderne." *Beauty Fashion,* December 1981, 54–60.

———. "Fragrance as an Art Form, Part V, Lalique by Himself." *Beauty Fashion,* January 1982, 46–49.

Cannell, David, and Sharon K. Christie. "Fragrance as an Art Form." *Beauty Fashion,* January 1979, 70–77.

Charabot, Dr. Eugene. "The City of Perfumes and Flowers [Grasse]." *Toilet Requisites,* June 1924, 56–58.

Clouzot, Henri. "Le Flaconnage Artistique Moderne." *La Renaissance de l'Art Français et des Industries de Luxe,* January 1919, 28–32.

Croissant, A. "The History of Perfumery." *Toilet Requisites,* November 1919.

Ellena, Jean-Claude. "Les Mots du Parfum." *Air France Atlas,* October 1987, 144–58.

The Fragrance Foundation. "Scents of Time: Reflections of Fragrance and Society." Handout at exhibition of same name touring the United States, October 1987–May 1989.

Hayot, Monelle. "Le Messager du Parfum: de la Bouteille de Senteur au Flacon d'Aujourd'hui." *L'Oeil,* July/August 1978, 42–49.

Janneau, Guillaume. "Le Mouvement Moderne: La Maison du Chevalier d'Orsay." *La Renaissance de l'Art Français et des Industries de Luxe,* March 1924, 133–39.

Meisler, Stanley. "In France, Perfume Is a Work of Art." *Los Angeles Times,* March 22, 1988, 1, 14–15.

"La Parfumerie aux Arts Décoratifs." *La Renaissance de l'Art Français et des Industries de Luxe,* July 1925.

"Société Anonyme des Parfums Arys." *La Parfumerie Française dans l'Art et la Présentation.* Paris: 1925.

153

A C K N O W L E D G M E N T S

154 THE FIRST RENÉ LALIQUE SPECIALIST DEALER, Mark Waller, owner of Galerie Moderne and prominent author on the subject, transformed the Utts' Lalique-collecting hobby into Mary Lou's grand passion for the "collection within the collection," the perfume bottles. This took place over many years, as it began when Mark was eighteen years old with a stand at London's Antiquarius, and is, no doubt, the principal reason this project was undertaken. He and his assistant, Martine de Cervens, have been of immeasurable help in gathering information, and particular appreciation is due Isobel Baker, formerly of the Galerie Moderne staff, for her professional collation of the data into a comprehensible form.

The personal interest of Marie-Claude Lalique has been inspiring as well as invaluable. The inclusion of her personal collection in this volume is a tribute to collectors everywhere. In addition, the cooperation of the entire Cristal Lalique staff in Paris (particularly Catherine Hyden and Odette Boulanger) and of Jacques Jugeat, Inc., in New York (Paul Lerner in particular) have made our task possible.

Nicholas M. Dawes, eminent author, dealer, and appraiser of Lalique and related Decorative Arts, has been of immeasureable help, as a friend and counselor, in bringing this project to fruition. Nick's knowledge of Lalique has been freely shared, as well as his many introductions to dealers, museums, and collectors—not to mention his instrumental role in contacts with Crown Publishers and with Cristal Lalique.

The suggestions and encouragement of other authors on the subject, particularly Katharine Morrison McClinton have been an important stimulus. McClinton is, of course, the author of the first important book on Lalique and has exchanged information and research with the authors for many years. Other authors whose help is gratefully acknowledged include: Hazel Martin, Jean Sloan, Jacquelyne Jones-North, and David Cannell in the United States, as well as Félix Marcilhac, Vivienne Becker, Sigrid Barten, and Victor Arwas in Europe.

In addition to Marie-Claude Lalique, private collectors of Lalique and of perfume bottles have been most generous in allowing us to view and catalog their rarities. These collectors include

Mr. and Mrs. Marvin Kagan, Mr. and Mrs. V. James Cole, Mr. and Mrs. R. Byron White, Dr. and Mrs. Edward F. Lewison, Mr. and Mrs. David Weinstein, Mr. and Mrs. Charles Magriel, Mr. and Mrs. Joel Shapiro, the late Dr. Kirby Shiffler and Mrs. Shiffler, as well as the Stanford Steppa, John Danis, Dorothy C. Shaker, Christie and Ed Lefkowith, Ken Leach and Richard J. Peters, Sali Blake, Priscilla McOstrich, Hazel Martin, Francis Touyarou-Grabe, Laurens and Lorraine Tartasky, Lippe-Waren and Tobias Collections.

Auction houses have supplied much material and guidance. In particular, we acknowledge Nicola Redway and Barbara Deisroth of Sotheby's; Nancy McClelland, Dan Klein, and Neil Froggatt of Christie's; Eric Knowles and Margaret Bishop of Bonhams; Hubert Le Blanc and Olivier Coutau-Bégarie of Hôtel Drouot; as well as Phillips and Butterfield and Butterfield.

The perfume companies have been most cooperative, and we would like to thank Coty (Marjorie Ambrogio), Nina Ricci (Caroline Crabbe and Freida Robinson), Worth (Sophie Raduis and Georges Bonnemaison), Roger et Gallet (Mr. Davy), and Molinard (Mr. Lerouge-Benard). In addition, we appreciate the assistance of The Fragrance Foundation (Annette Green), sponsor of the exhibition "Scents of Time" (1987–1989).

Dealers in Lalique and the Art Deco period, as well as those specializing in perfume bottles, have been of immeasurable help. Aside from Nicholas Dawes, these include Lillian Nassau, Primavera, Bizarre Bazaar Ltd., Gallery 47, Madeleine France Antiques, Crystal Galleries, and Robert Zehil Galleries in the United States; Galerie Moderne, Gallery 25, Pruskin Gallery, John Jesse, Editions Graphiques Gallery in London; Beauté Divine, Danenberg & Cie, and Félix Marcilhac in Paris; Michel Philippe at the Marché Rosiers/Biron in the "Flea Market" at Saint-Ouen; as well as Kiya Gallery (Ichiro Kato) in Tokyo and Sanjyo Gion Gallery (Mr. Kajikawa) in Kyoto.

Museums deserve a special mention, including the Metropolitan Museum of Art (Craig Miller), Musée des Arts Décoratifs (Yvonne Brunhammer), Musée International de la Parfumerie (Georges Vindry and Joëlle Dejardin), Los Angeles County Museum of Art (Timothy Schroder), and Museum of the City of New York (Deborah Shinn, curator of "Scents of Time"). In addition, we would like to thank Mr. Jean-Jacques Vignault (*Président d'Honneur* of La Federation Française de La Parfumerie) for his kind consultations.

Finally we would note the able assistance of our typist, Sharon Bradford, and the help of the Information on Demand, Inc., organization in locating rare literature and advertisements.

COLLECTION CREDITS

◆

Collection Marie-Claude Lalique.
Figures 7, 9, 10, 11, 12, 30, 33, 41, 58, 68, 69, 70, 75, 81, 88, 91, 94, 106, 109, 114, 122, 123, 130, 131, 139, 141, 168, 170, 172, 178, 184, 185, 186, 196, 197, 203, 206, 207, 209, 218, 221, 223, 226, 234.

Courtesy Cristal Lalique.
Figures 5, 65, 79, 244, 245, 246, 247, 249, 250, 251, 252, 253, 254, 255, 256, 257.

Collection Mary Lou Utt.
Figures 17, 19, 20, 22, 24, 25, 29, 31, 39, 40, 49, 61, 62, 67, 71, 72, 73, 80, 82, 86, 96, 98, 100, 104, 107, 108, 112, 113, 124, 135, 143, 144, 150, 153, 166, 169, 171, 173, 175, 182, 190, 191, 193, 199, 200, 202, 213, 214, 217, 220.

Collection Glenn and Mary Lou Utt.
Figures 2, 4, 90.

Private French Collection.
Figures 21, 32, 56, 76, 77, 78, 105, 115, 116, 125, 149, 155, 156, 157, 174, 177, 198, 201, 208, 227.

Galerie Moderne, London.
Figures 1, 6, 18, 83, 85, 89, 134, 152, 161, 162, 163, 179, 210.

Courtesy Nicholas M. Dawes.
Figures 13, 59, 60, 64, 97, 129, 212.

Courtesy Régine de Robien, Paris.
Figures 15, 95, 133, 136, 138, 224, 233.

Courtesy Régine de Robien Olivier Contau-Bégarie, Paris.
Figures 34, 99, 204, 230.

Madeleine France, Plantation, Florida.
Figures 126, 127, 146, 158, 231, 236.

Collection Ken Leach/Richard J. Peters.
Figures 132, 181, 194, 195, 211.

Collection Hazel Martin.
Figures 225, 240, 241, 242.

Musée des Arts Décoratifs, Paris.
Figures 14, 16, 23, 27, 102.

Courtesy John Danis.
Figures 142, 145, 147, 188.

Collection Touyarou-Grabe.
Figures 118, 151, 183, 192.

Collection Dorothy C. Shaker.
Figures 176, 180, 219.

Jacquelyne Jones-North.
Figures 158, 189, 222.

Kagan Collection.
Figures 28, 160.

Bonhams, London.
Figures 110, 243.

Crystal Galleries, Boulder, Colorado.
Figures 8, 101.

Weinstein Collection.
Figures 205, 215.

Courtesy Parfums Worth, Paris.
Figures 140, 229.

Courtesy Félix Marcilhac/Hubert Le Blanc, Paris.
Figures 128, 159.

Courtesy Bizarre Bazaar Ltd., New York.
Figures 93, 95.

Sotheby's, London.
Figure 258.

Musée International de la Perfumerie, Grasse.
Figure 216.

Courtesy Nina Ricci.
Figure 235.

Phillips, New York.
Figure 119.

Molinard Collection, Grasse.
Figure 164.

Collection Lillian Nassau.
Figure 3.

Collection Mrs. Edward F. Lewison.
Figure 103.

Collection Mr. and Mrs. V. James Cole.
Figure 84.

Collection Stanford Steppa.
Figure 74.

PHOTOGRAPH CREDITS
———— ◆ ————

Photographs by Andrew Stewart, London:
Figures 1, 6, 17, 18, 21, 28, 32, 56, 76, 77, 78, 83, 85,
89, 105, 115, 116, 125, 134, 137, 149, 150, 152, 155,
156, 157, 160, 161, 162, 163, 174, 177, 179, 198, 201,
208, 227.

Photographs by Ralph Cowan Studio, Chicago:
Figures 22, 25, 26, 39, 40, 44, 45, 46, 49, 62, 63, 67,
82, 96, 98, 107, 108, 113, 144, 147, 148, 153, 166, 182,
191, 210, 248.

Photographs by Nelson Tiffany & Associates,
Palm Desert, CA:
Figures 45, 61, 71, 72, 90, 95, 104, 112, 123, 124, 158,
171, 173, 175, 190, 193, 200, 225, 228, 231, 236, 239.

Photographs by Peter Brenner Photography,
Burbank, CA:
Figures 2, 19, 20, 24, 29, 31, 64, 73, 86, 100, 120, 121,
135, 142, 143, 154, 165, 169, 199, 202, 220, 237.

Photographs by Kevin J. Heinbuch, Perkins Studios,
Minocqua, WI:
Figures 74, 84, 93, 103, 111, 117, 122, 126, 127, 180,
185, 217, 224, 238.

Photographs by Terry McGinniss, New York City:
Figures 4, 59, 60, 97, 129, 212, 213, 214.

Photographs by Dennis Lee, Indio, CA:
Figures 43, 50, 80, 145, 167, 187, 188.

Photographs by Philippe Doumic, Paris:
Figures 15, 133, 136, 138, 233.

Photographs by Elizabeth A. McCarron,
New York City:
Figures 132, 181, 194, 195, 211.

Photographs by permission Musée des
Arts Décoratifs, Paris:
Figures 14, 16, 23, 27, 102.

Photographs by Roland Dreysus, Paris:
Figures 34, 99, 204, 230.

Photographs by Nefcam Photography, Methuen, MA:
Figures 176, 219.

Photographs by Benko Photography, Boulder, CO:
Figures 8, 101.

Photograph by Jacques Mayer Photographe,
Grasse, France:
Figure 216.

Photograph by Sing-Si Swartz, New York City:
Figure 3.

Photograph by Photo Appollot, Grasse, France:
Figure 164.

INDEX

158

160